The Song of Hiawatha

A Majestic Native-American Legend of Nature, Heroism & Spirit

A Modern Translation
Adapted for the Contemporary Reader

Henry W. Longfellow

Translated by Tim Zengerink

Table of Contents

Preface Message to the Reader.. 1

Introduction 2

Preface 7

Chapter I: The Peace-Pipe 10

Chapter II: The Four Winds.. 16

Chapter III: Hiawatha's Childhood 25

Chapter IV: Hiawatha and Mudjekeewis 32

Chapter V: Hiawatha's Fasting... 42

Chapter VI: Hiawatha's Friends.. 51

Chapter VII: Hiawatha's Sailing... 56

Chapter VIII: Hiawatha's Fishing... 61

Chapter IX: Hiawatha and the Pearl-Feather...................... 68

Chapter X: Hiawatha's Wooing 77

Chapter XI: Hiawatha's Wedding-Feast 86

Chapter XII: The Son of the Evening Star 94

Chapter XIII: Blessing the Cornfields................................. 105

Chapter XIV: Picture-Writing 113

Chapter XV: Hiawatha's Lamentation 118

Chapter XVI: Pau-Puk-Keewis 125

Chapter XVII: The Hunting of Pau-Puk-Keewis................. 133

Chapter XVIII: The Death of Kwasind................................. 145

Chapter XIX: The Ghosts 149

Chapter XX: The Famine 156

Chapter XXI: The White Man's Foot 161

Chapter XXII: Hiawatha's Departure 169

Thank You For Reading 181

Preface
Message to the Reader

Rebuilding the Greatest Library in Human History

Thousands of years ago, the Library of Alexandria was the heart of global knowledge — a sanctuary where the wisdom of every known civilization was gathered and shared freely.

And then, it was lost.

Now, we're rebuilding it — and you are invited to join us.

At the Library of Alexandria, we've set out to make every book available to every person on Earth — not just in print, but in every language, every format, and for every reader.

Here's how we do it:

- **Deluxe Print Editions at True Printing Cost** - Order any book as a high-quality paperback, elegant hardcover, or stunning boxset — and only pay what it costs to print. No markups. No middlemen.
- **Unlimited Access to the Greatest Works** - Enjoy thousands of timeless classics — from Plato to Shakespeare to Tolstoy — in beautiful, modern eBook and audiobook editions. Read and listen without limits — for every reader, everywhere.
- **Modern Translations for Every Language & Dialect** - We're reimagining the classics in clear, accessible language — and translating them into every dialect imaginable. Everyone deserves to understand humanity's greatest ideas.

When you visit **LibraryofAlexandria.com**, you're not just accessing books — you're joining a global movement to restore, preserve, and share the wisdom of civilization.

Join us today at LibraryofAlexandria.com

Together, we'll ensure the light of human wisdom never fades again.

With gratitude,

The Modern Library of Alexandria Team

Visit:
www.libraryofalexandria.com
Or scan the code below:

Introduction

Longfellow's Vision and the Birth of an American Epic

Henry Wadsworth Longfellow's *The Song of Hiawatha* (1855) is one of the most celebrated and ambitious works of 19th-century American literature, a sweeping narrative poem that seeks to capture the spiritual grandeur, cultural traditions, and heroic ideals of Native American life. Written in a trochaic tetrameter inspired by the Finnish epic Kalevala, Longfellow's poem is both a work of artistic innovation and a cultural landmark. It attempts to forge an epic rooted in the New World, rather than drawing exclusively on European mythologies and traditions, and in doing so, it helped to shape an emerging American literary identity.

The poem is set in a mythic, pre-colonial America, focusing on the titular hero, Hiawatha, who embodies the virtues of strength, wisdom, and harmony with nature. Through a series of episodic tales, Longfellow weaves together a narrative that celebrates not only the heroic deeds of Hiawatha but also the interconnectedness of the natural and spiritual worlds. The poem draws heavily on Native American legends, particularly those of the Ojibwe and other Algonquian peoples, though it is filtered through Longfellow's Romantic sensibilities and his desire to create a universal epic that would resonate with both American and European audiences.

Longfellow's choice to write in a rhythmic, incantatory meter gives *The Song of Hiawatha* a distinctive musical quality, one that echoes oral traditions and the cadence of storytelling. This stylistic decision, coupled with his rich imagery and deep reverence for the natural world, allows the poem to evoke a sense of timelessness and spiritual depth. The work is both a celebration of Native

American culture and a Romantic meditation on humanity's relationship with nature, the divine, and the cycles of life and death.

Published at a time when America was grappling with questions of national identity and cultural independence, *The Song of Hiawatha* was both a literary success and a cultural phenomenon. It sold thousands of copies upon its release and quickly became a staple of American poetry. While modern readers may approach the poem with greater sensitivity to issues of cultural representation and appropriation, its historical importance and artistic ambition remain undeniable. Longfellow sought to honor the oral traditions and spiritual wisdom of Native peoples, even as his work reflects the 19th-century lens through which he viewed them.

Themes of Heroism, Nature, and Spiritual Harmony

One of the central themes of *The Song of Hiawatha* is the ideal of heroic leadership. Hiawatha is portrayed not only as a warrior and hunter but also as a wise teacher and spiritual guide. His deeds are not merely acts of physical strength but demonstrations of moral and communal responsibility. Longfellow's Hiawatha is a figure who unites his people, fosters peace, and lives in harmony with the natural world—a vision of leadership that contrasts with the industrial and often destructive values of 19th-century Western society.

Nature plays an equally important role in the poem. The landscapes of rivers, forests, lakes, and skies are described with vivid detail and reverence, reflecting Longfellow's Romantic belief that nature is both a source of spiritual wisdom and a mirror of the human soul. The natural world in *The Song of Hiawatha* is not merely a backdrop but an active participant in the narrative. Animals, plants, and natural forces are imbued with personality and agency, often guiding or testing Hiawatha on his journey. This animistic worldview aligns with many Native traditions, in which the natural world is seen as alive, interconnected, and sacred.

The spiritual dimension of the poem is equally profound. Longfellow draws upon Native American myths of creation, transformation, and the afterlife, presenting them in a way that emphasizes universal themes of life, death, and rebirth. Hiawatha's journey is as much a spiritual quest as it is a series of heroic exploits. He learns to listen to the wisdom of the elders, to respect the spirits of the land and the ancestors, and to see himself as part of a greater cosmic order. Through these elements, Longfellow crafts a narrative that transcends its historical and cultural setting to explore the fundamental questions of human existence.

Another recurring theme in the poem is the tension between tradition and change. Hiawatha's story unfolds during a time of transition, when old ways of life are being challenged by new forces, both natural and human. This tension is reflected in the poem's episodic structure, which moves from tales of childhood and love to stories of conflict, reconciliation, and ultimately, departure. By the end of the poem, Hiawatha sails westward into the sunset, symbolically departing from his people but leaving behind a legacy of wisdom and unity.

Longfellow's Style and Cultural Impact

Longfellow's style in *The Song of Hiawatha* is characterized by its rhythmic regularity, vivid imagery, and lyrical simplicity. The trochaic meter, with its strong, falling rhythm, lends the poem a chant-like quality that evokes oral storytelling traditions. This meter, borrowed from the Finnish Kalevala, was a daring choice for an American epic, as it broke with the iambic patterns commonly used in English poetry. The result is a work that feels both ancient and innovative, blending the cadence of traditional epics with the sensibilities of 19th-century Romanticism.

The imagery of the poem is equally powerful. Longfellow's descriptions of the natural world are rich with color, texture, and movement, creating a vivid and immersive reading experience. His portrayal of the seasons, the landscapes of the Great Lakes region, and the daily lives of Hiawatha's people are infused with both realism and a sense of mythic grandeur. At the same time, Longfellow's language is accessible, avoiding the ornate diction of some of his contemporaries in favor of a style that feels direct and musical.

Upon its publication, *The Song of Hiawatha* was met with widespread acclaim, though it was not without its critics. Some accused Longfellow of romanticizing Native American culture or of appropriating its legends for a primarily white readership. Others, however, praised the poem for introducing American audiences to the richness and beauty of indigenous traditions, even if through a Romanticized lens. Today, the poem is often studied not only as a work of art but also as a cultural artifact, reflecting 19th-century attitudes toward Native peoples as well as the complexities of cross-cultural representation.

The cultural impact of *The Song of Hiawatha* extends far beyond literature. The poem inspired music (most notably Antonín Dvořák's "New World Symphony"), visual art, and even popular culture, shaping the way many Americans of the 19th and 20th centuries imagined Native American life. While modern readers approach the poem with a greater awareness of its limitations and biases, it remains an important part of the American literary canon, both for its artistic achievements and for its role in shaping national identity.

For readers today, *The Song of Hiawatha* offers an opportunity to engage with a work that is at once beautiful, flawed, and deeply meaningful. It invites reflection on the ways in which stories shape our understanding of culture, history, and the natural world. Longfellow's vision, while rooted in his own time, speaks to universal themes of heroism, love, loss, and the quest for harmony with the forces that govern life and death.

The Song of Hiawatha

Preface

Should you ask me where these stories come from?
Where do these legends and traditions come from,
With the scents of the forest
With the dew and moisture of the meadows,
With the curling smoke rising from wigwams,
With the rushing of great rivers,
With their constant repetitions,
And their wild reverberations
As of thunder in the mountains?
I should respond, I should tell you,
"From the forests and the prairies,
From the vast lakes of the northern territories,
From the land of the Ojibways,
From the land of the Dakotas,
From the mountains, moorlands, and marshlands
Where the heron, the Shuh-shuh-gah,
Feeds among the reeds and rushes.
I'm sharing them exactly as they were told to me
From the lips of Nawadaha,
"The musician, the sweet singer."
Should you ask where Nawadaha
Found these songs so wild and untamed,
Found these legends and traditions,
I should respond, I should tell you,
"In the bird's nests of the forest,"
In the beaver lodges,
In the hoofprint of the bison,
In the eagle's nest!

"All the wild birds sang to him,"
In the moorlands and the marshlands,
In the gloomy swamplands;
Chetowaik, the plover, sang them,
Mahng, the loon, the wild goose, Wawa,
The blue heron, the Shuh-shuh-gah,
"And the grouse, the Mushkodasa!"
If you were to ask me even further,
Saying, "Who was Nawadaha?"
"Tell us about this Nawadaha,"
I should respond to your questions.
Immediately in the following words.
"In the valley of Tawasentha,
In the green and quiet valley,
By the delightful streams,
The singer Nawadaha lived there.
Around the Indian village
Spread the meadows and the cornfields,
And beyond them stood the forest,
The groves of singing pine trees stood there,
Green in summer, white in winter,
Ever sighing, ever singing.
"And the delightful streams,"
You could follow their path through the valley,
By the rushing waters in springtime,
By the alder trees in the summer,
By the white fog in the autumn,
By the black line in the winter;
And beside them lived the singer,
In the valley of Tawasentha,
In the green and quiet valley.
"There he sang of Hiawatha,"
Sang the Song of Hiawatha,

Sang of his miraculous birth and existence,
How he prayed and how he fasted,
How he lived, worked hard, and endured hardship,
That human tribes might flourish,
"That he might advance his people!"
You who love the places where Nature dwells,
Love the sunshine of the meadow,
Love the shadow of the forest,
Love the wind among the branches,
And the rainstorm and the snowstorm,
And the rushing of great rivers
Through their fences of pine trees,
And the thunder in the mountains,
Whose countless echoes
Soar like eagles in their mountain nests;--
Listen to these extraordinary stories,
To this Song of Hiawatha!
You who love a nation's legends,
Love the folk songs of a people,
That like voices from afar off
Call to us to pause and listen,
Speak in tones so plain and childlike,
Barely can the ear tell the difference
Whether they are sung or spoken;--
Listen to this Indian Legend,
To this Song of Hiawatha!
You whose hearts are fresh and simple,
Who have faith in God and Nature,
Who believe that throughout all eras
Every human heart is human,
That even in the hearts of savages
There are longings, yearnings, and strivings
For they do not understand what is good,

That weak hands and those who are helpless,
Fumbling helplessly through the darkness,
Touch God's right hand in that darkness
And are lifted up and strengthened;--
Listen to this simple story,
To this Song of Hiawatha!
You, who sometimes, in your wanderings
Through the green country lanes,
Where the twisted barberry bushes grow
Hang their clusters of bright red berries
Over gray stone walls covered with moss,
Pause by some forgotten cemetery,
For a while to reflect and contemplate
On a partially erased inscription,
Written with little skill in the art of songwriting,
Everyday expressions, but each letter
Full of hope and yet heartbroken,
Full of all the gentle emotion
Of the Here and the Hereafter;
Stay and read this rough inscription,
Read this Song of Hiawatha!

———————

Chapter I:
The Peace-Pipe

On the Mountains of the Prairie,
On the Great Red Pipestone Quarry,
Gitche Manito, the mighty,
He, the Master of Life, descending,
On the red cliffs of the quarry
Stood upright, and summoned the nations,

Called the tribes of humanity together.
From his footprints flowed a river,
Jumped into the bright morning light,
Over the precipice plunging downward
Gleamed like Ishkoodah, the comet.
And the Spirit, bending down toward the earth,
With his finger on the meadow
Carved out a twisting route for it,
"Run this way!" he told it.
From the red stone of the quarry
With his hand he broke off a piece,
Shaped it into a pipe bowl,
Shaped and crafted it with figures;
From the riverbank
Took a long reed to use as a pipe stem,
With its dark green leaves covering it;
Filled the pipe with willow bark,
With the bark of the red willow;
Breathed upon the neighboring forest,
Made its massive branches rub against each other,
Until they burst into flames and ignited;
And standing tall upon the mountains,
Gitche Manito, the mighty,
Smoked the calumet, the Peace-Pipe,
As a signal to the nations.
And the smoke drifted upward slowly, slowly,
Through the peaceful morning air,
First a single line of darkness,
Then a thicker, deeper blue mist appeared,
Then a snow-white cloud began to unfold,
Like the treetops of the forest,
Ever rising, rising, rising,
Until it reached the highest point of heaven,

Until it shattered against the sky,
And spread outward in all directions around it.
From the Valley of Tawasentha,
From the Valley of Wyoming,
From the groves of Tuscaloosa,
From the distant Rocky Mountains,
From the Northern lakes and rivers
All the tribes saw the signal,
Saw the distant smoke rising,
The Pukwana of the Peace-Pipe.
And the Prophets of the nations
Said: "Look at it, the Pukwana!"
By the signal of the Peace Pipe,
Bending like a willow branch,
Waving like a hand that beckons,
Gitche Manito, the mighty,
Calls the tribes of humanity together,
"Calls the warriors to his council!"
Down the rivers, across the prairies,
The warriors of the nations came,
The Delawares and Mohawks arrived,
The Choctaws and Comanches came,
The Shoshonies and Blackfeet came,
The Pawnees and Omahas came,
The Mandans and Dakotas came,
The Hurons and Ojibways came,
All the warriors gathered together
By the signal of the Peace Pipe,
To the Mountains of the Prairie,
To the Great Red Pipestone Quarry,
And they stood there on the meadow,
With their weapons and their battle equipment,
Painted like the leaves of autumn,

Painted like the sky of morning,
Staring at each other with wild intensity;
In their faces stern defiance,
In their hearts lie the conflicts that have lasted for generations,
The inherited hatred,
The ancestral thirst for revenge.
Gitche Manito, the mighty,
The creator of the nations,
Looked at them with compassion,
With fatherly love and compassion;
Witnessed their anger and quarreling
But just like arguments between children,
But like the petty quarrels and squabbles of children!
Over them he extended his right hand,
To overcome their resistant personalities,
To ease their thirst and fever,
By the shadow of his right hand;
Spoke to them with a majestic voice
As the sound of distant waters,
Plunging into profound depths,
Warning and scolding, spoke in this way:
"Oh my children! My poor children!"
Listen to these words of wisdom,
Listen to these words of warning,
From the lips of the Great Spirit,
From the Master of Life, who created you!
"I have given you lands to hunt in,"
I have provided you with streams where you can fish,
I have given you bear and bison,
I have given you fish eggs and reindeer,
I have given you brant and beaver,
Filled the marshes with waterfowl,
Filled the rivers full of fish:

Why aren't you satisfied then?
Why then will you hunt each other?
"I am tired of your arguments,"
Tired of your conflicts and violence,
Tired of your prayers for revenge,
Of your arguments and conflicts;
All your power lies in your unity,
All your danger lies in discord;
Therefore, be at peace from now on.
And as brothers live together.
"I will send a Prophet to you,"
A Deliverer of the nations,
Who will guide you and teach you,
Who will work hard and endure hardship alongside you.
If you follow his advice,
You will multiply and prosper;
If his warnings are ignored,
You will fade away and perish!
"Bathe now in the stream before you,
Wash the war paint from your faces.
Wash the bloodstains from your fingers,
Bury your war-clubs and your weapons,
Break the red stone from this quarry,
Mold and shape it into Peace-Pipes,
Take the reeds that grow beside you,
Adorn them with your most brilliant plumage,
Smoke the peace pipe together,
"And let us live as brothers from now on!"
Then the warriors fell to the ground
Threw their cloaks and deerskin shirts,
Threw their weapons and their war equipment,
Jumped into the fast-flowing river,
Washed the war-paint from their faces.

Clear above them flowed the water,
Clear and transparent from the footprints
Of the Master of Life descending;
Dark water flowed beneath them,
Dirty and marked with streaks of red,
As if blood were mixed with it!
From the river came the warriors,
Clean and washed free of all their war paint;
On the shores they buried their war clubs,
Buried all their warlike weapons.
Gitche Manito, the mighty,
The Great Spirit, the creator,
Smiled upon his helpless children!
And in silence all the warriors
Broke the red stone of the quarry,
Smoothed and shaped it into Peace-Pipes,
Broke the long reeds by the river,
Adorned them with their most brilliant plumage,
And each person went home,
While the Master of Life was rising,
Through the parting of the cloudy veils,
Through the doorways of heaven,
Vanished from before their faces,
In the smoke that swirled around him,
The Pukwana of the Peace-Pipe!

———————

Chapter II:
The Four Winds

"Honor be to Mudjekeewis!"
The warriors cried out, the old men cried out,
When he returned home in triumph
With the sacred Belt of Wampum,
From the northern regions where the cold winds blow,
From the kingdom of Wabasso,
From the land of the White Rabbit.
He had stolen the Belt of Wampum
From the neck of Mishe-Mokwa,
From the Great Bear of the mountains,
From the terror of the nations,
As he lay sleeping heavily
On the summit of the mountains,
Like a rock covered with moss,
Spotted brown and gray with mosses.
Quietly he crept up on him
Until the crimson claws of the beast
Almost reached him, almost frightened him,
Until the hot breath from his nostrils
Warmed the hands of Mudjekeewis,
As he pulled the Belt of Wampum
Over the round ears that could not hear,
Over the small eyes that could not see,
Over the long nose and nostrils,
The dark covering of the nostrils,
Out of which came the labored breathing
Warmed the hands of Mudjekeewis.
Then he raised his war club high above his head,
Shouted his war cry loud and long,

Struck down the mighty Mishe-Mokwa
In the center of the forehead,
Right between the eyes he struck him.
With the heavy blow bewildered,
Rose the Great Bear of the mountains;
But his knees trembled beneath him,
And he whimpered like a woman,
As he stumbled and lurched forward,
As he sat on his hind legs;
And the mighty Mudjekeewis,
Standing fearlessly before him,
Mocked him with loud scorn,
Spoke disdainfully in this way:
"Listen here, Bear! You are a coward;"
And you're no brave warrior, as you claimed to be;
Unless you would not cry and whimper
Like a miserable woman!
Bear! You know our tribes are enemies.
Long have they been at war together;
Now you discover that we are at our most powerful,
You go sneaking through the forest,
You go hiding in the mountains!
Had you defeated me in combat
Not a single groan would I have made;
But you, Bear! sit here and cry,
And bring shame to your people by weeping,
Like a miserable Shaugodaya,
"Like a cowardly old woman!"
Then he lifted his war club again,
Struck the Mishe-Mokwa once more
In the middle of his forehead,
Broke his skull, as ice is broken
When someone goes fishing in winter.

Thus was slain the Mishe-Mokwa,
He the Great Bear of the mountains,
He was the terror of the nations.
"Honor be to Mudjekeewis!"
With a shout, the people exclaimed,
"Honor be to Mudjekeewis!"
From now on, he will be the West Wind.
And from now on and forever
Shall he hold supreme dominion
Over all the winds of heaven.
Call him Mudjekeewis no more,
"Call him Kabeyun, the West-Wind!"
Thus, Mudjekeewis was chosen
Father of the Winds of Heaven.
For himself he kept the West Wind,
Gave the others to his children;
To Wabun he gave the East Wind,
Gave the South to Shawondasee,
And the North Wind, wild and cruel,
To the fierce Kabibonokka.
Young and beautiful was Wabun;
He was the one who brought the morning,
He was the one whose silver arrows
Chased the darkness over hill and valley;
He was the one whose cheeks were painted
With the most brilliant streaks of crimson,
And whose voice awakened the village,
Called the deer, and called the hunter.
Wabun was alone in the sky;
Though the birds sang cheerfully to him,
Though the wildflowers of the meadow
Filled the air with fragrances for him;
Though the forests and the rivers

Sang and shouted at his coming,
Still his heart was heavy with sadness,
For he was alone in heaven.
But one morning, looking down at the earth,
While the village was still sleeping,
And the fog settled over the river,
Like a ghost that disappears at sunrise,
He saw a young woman walking
All alone in a meadow,
Collecting water lilies and reeds
By a river in the meadow.
Every morning, looking down at the earth,
Still the first thing he saw there
Was she looking at him with her blue eyes,
Two blue lakes nestled among the tall reeds.
And he loved the lonely maiden,
Who waited like this for his arrival;
For they were both alone,
She on earth and he in heaven.
And he courted her with tender touches,
Wooed her with his radiant smile,
With his charming words, he courted her,
With his sighing and his singing,
Gentle whispers in the branches,
Softest music, sweetest odors,
Until he pulled her close to his chest,
Wrapped in his crimson robes,
Until he transformed her into a star,
Trembling still upon his chest;
And forever in the heavens
They are seen walking together.
Wabun and the Wabun-Annung,
Wabun and the Morning Star.

But the fierce Kabibonokka
Had his home among icebergs,
In the endless snowdrifts,
In the kingdom of Wabasso,
In the land of the White Rabbit.
He was the one whose hand in autumn
Painted all the trees with scarlet,
Stained the leaves with red and yellow;
He was the one who sent the snowflake,
Whistling and hissing through the forest,
Froze the ponds, the lakes, the rivers,
Drove the loon and seagull southward,
Drove away the cormorant and curlew
To their nests made of sedge grass and seaweed
In the lands of Shawondasee.
Once the fierce Kabibonokka
Emerging from his shelter made of snow-drifts
From his home among the icebergs,
And his hair, sprinkled with snow,
Flowed behind him like a river,
Like a dark and wintry river,
As he cried out and rushed toward the south,
Over frozen lakes and moorlands.
There among the reeds and rushes
Found he Shingebis, the diver,
Dragging lines of fish behind him,
Across the frozen marshes and moorlands,
Remaining still among the moorlands,
Though his people had long since left
To the land of Shawondasee.
Cried the fierce Kabibonokka,
"Who is this that dares to challenge me?"
Dares to remain in my territory,

When the Wawa has departed,
When the wild goose has flown south,
And the heron, the Shuh-shuh-gah,
Long ago departed southward?
I will enter his dwelling.
"I will put out his smoldering fire!"
And at night Kabibonokka,
To the lodge came wild and wailing,
The snow piled up in drifts around it,
Shouted down into the smoke-flue,
Shook the lodge-poles in his fury,
The curtain in the doorway fluttered.
Shingebis, the diver, was not afraid,
Shingebis, the diver, didn't care;
Four large logs served as his firewood.
One for each moon of the winter,
And the fish provided him with food.
By his blazing fire he sat there,
Warm and cheerful, eating, laughing,
Singing, "O Kabibonokka,
"You are just a fellow human being like me!"
Then Kabibonokka entered,
And although Shingebis, the diver,
Felt his presence by the coldness,
Felt his icy breath upon him,
Still he did not stop his singing,
Still he did not stop his laughing,
Only turned the log a little,
Only made the fire burn brighter,
Made the sparks fly up the chimney.
From Kabibonokka's forehead,
From his snow-covered hair,
Beads of sweat dropped quickly and heavily,

Making impressions in the ashes,
As along the eaves of lodges,
As from the drooping branches of hemlock,
The melting snow drips in springtime,
Making hollows in the snowdrifts.
Until finally he stood up, defeated,
Could not tolerate the heat and laughter,
Could not tolerate the cheerful singing,
But rushed headlong through the doorway,
Imprinted on the hardened snow drifts,
Imprinted on the lakes and rivers,
Made the snow on top of them more solid,
Made the ice covering them thicker,
Shingebis, the diver, was challenged,
To step forward and grapple with him,
To step forward and fight without protection
On the frozen wetlands and moorlands.
Shingebis the diver went forth,
Wrestled all night with the North Wind,
Wrestled naked on the moorlands
With the fierce Kabibonokka,
Until his labored breathing became weaker,
Until his icy grip became weaker,
Until he swayed and stumbled backward,
And pulled back, confused and defeated,
To the kingdom of Wabasso,
To the land of the White Rabbit,
Hearing still the gusty laughter,
Hearing Shingebis, the diver,
Singing, "O Kabibonokka,
"You are just a fellow human being like me!"
Shawondasee, fat and lazy,
Had his home far to the south,

In the sleepy, dreamlike sunshine,
In the endless Summer.
He was the one who sent the wood-birds,
Sent the robin, the Opechee,
Sent the bluebird, the Owaissa,
Sent the Shawshaw, sent the swallow,
Sent the wild goose, Wawa, northward,
Sent the melons and tobacco,
And the grapes in purple clusters.
From his pipe the smoke rose upward
Filled the sky with haze and vapor,
Filled the air with dreamy softness,
Gave a sparkle to the water,
Touched the rugged hills with smoothness,
Brought the gentle Indian Summer
To the melancholy north-land,
In the bleak Moon of Snowshoes.
Listless, careless Shawondasee!
In his life he had one shadow,
In his heart, he carried one sorrow.
Once, while he was looking toward the north,
Far away on a prairie
He saw a young woman standing there.
Saw a tall and slender maiden
All alone on a prairie;
Brightest green were all her garments,
And her hair was like the sunshine.
Day by day he looked at her,
Day by day he sighed with passion,
Day by day his heart within him
Burned even more intensely with love and desire
For the maid with golden hair.
But he was too overweight and lazy

To rouse himself and court her.
Yes, too lazy and comfortable
To chase after her and convince her;
So he simply looked at her,
Only sat and sighed with deep emotion
For the maiden of the prairie.
Until one morning, looking toward the north,
He gazed upon her golden hair.
Changed and covered over with whiteness,
Covered as with the whitest snowflakes.
"Ah! my brother from the North-land,
From the kingdom of Wabasso,
From the land of the White Rabbit!
You have taken the young woman away from me,
You have placed your hand upon her,
You have courted and won my young woman,
"With your stories of the North-land!"
Thus the miserable Shawondasee
Breathed his sorrow into the air;
And the South Wind across the prairie
Wandered warm with sighs of passion,
With the sighs of Shawondasee,
Until the air appeared filled with snowflakes,
Full of thistle-down the prairie,
And the maid with hair like sunshine
Vanished from his sight forever;
Never again did Shawondasee
See the maid with golden hair!
Poor, deluded Shawondasee!
It wasn't a woman that you were looking at,
It wasn't a maiden that you longed for,
It was the prairie dandelion
That throughout the entire dreamlike summer

You had looked at with such deep yearning,
You had longed for with such intense desire,
And had vanished forever,
Blown into the air with sighing.
Ah! deceived Shawondasee!
Thus the Four Winds were divided
Thus the sons of Mudjekeewis
Had their positions in the heavens,
At the corners of the heavens;
For himself alone the West Wind
Kept the mighty Mudjekeewis.

Chapter III:
Hiawatha's Childhood

Through the evening twilight, descending downward,
In the days that have been forgotten,
In the forgotten ages,
From the full moon fell Nokomis,
Fell the beautiful Nokomis,
She is a wife, but not a mother.
She was playing with her female companions.
Swinging in a swing made of grapevines,
When she rejected her rival,
Full of jealousy and hatred,
Cut the leafy swing apart,
Cut the twisted grapevines in half,
And Nokomis fell terrified
Through the evening twilight, descending downward,
On the Muskoday, the meadow,
On the prairie full of blossoms.

"Look! A star is falling!" the people said;
"A star is falling from the sky!"
There among the ferns and mosses,
There among the prairie lilies,
On the Muskoday, the meadow,
In the moonlight and the starlight,
Fair Nokomis gave birth to a daughter.
And she gave her the name Wenonah,
As the eldest of her daughters.
And the daughter of Nokomis
Grew up like the prairie lilies,
Grew into a tall and slender young woman,
With the beauty of the moonlight,
With the beauty of the starlight.
And Nokomis warned her often,
Saying often, and often repeating,
"Oh, beware of Mudjekeewis,
Of the West Wind, Mudjekeewis;
Listen not to what he tells you;
Do not lie down upon the meadow,
Stoop not down among the lilies,
"Don't let the West Wind come and hurt you!"
But she paid no attention to the warning,
Ignored those wise words,
And the West Wind arrived in the evening,
Walking gently across the prairie,
Whispering to the leaves and blossoms,
Bending low the flowers and grasses,
Found the beautiful Wenonah,
Lying there among the lilies,
Courted her with his sweet words,
Courted her with his gentle touches,
Until she gave birth to a son in sorrow,

Gave birth to a son born of both love and sorrow.
Thus was born my Hiawatha,
Thus was born the child of wonder;
But the daughter of Nokomis,
Hiawatha's gentle mother,
In her suffering, she died alone and abandoned.
By the West Wind, deceitful and unfaithful,
By the heartless Mudjekeewis.
For her daughter long and loudly
Nokomis cried out in sorrow and wept bitterly;
"If only I were dead!" she whispered.
"Oh, if only I were dead, as you are!"
No more work, and no more weeping,
"Wahonowin! Wahonowin!"
By the shores of Gitche Gumee,
By the gleaming Great Water,
Stood the wigwam of Nokomis,
Daughter of the Moon, Nokomis.
Dark behind it rose the forest,
Rose the dark and somber pine trees,
Rose the fir trees with their cones;
Bright before it, the water sparkled.
Beat the clear and sunny water,
Beat the shining Big-Sea-Water.
There the wrinkled old Nokomis
Nursed the little Hiawatha,
Gently swayed him in his basswood cradle,
Nestled gently in moss and reeds,
Securely tied with reindeer tendons;
Calmed his restless crying by saying,
"Quiet! The Naked Bear will hear you!"
Sang him gently to sleep,
"Ewa-yea! my little owlet!"

Who is this person that illuminates the wigwam?
With his bright eyes, does he light up the wigwam?
"Ewa-yea! my little owlet!"
Many things Nokomis taught him
Of the stars that shine in heaven;
Showed him Ishkoodah, the comet,
Ishkoodah, with fiery hair;
Revealed the Death-Dance of the spirits,
Warriors wearing their feathers and carrying their war clubs,
Blazing brightly in the distant north
In the cold winter nights;
Revealed the wide white path in heaven,
Pathway of the ghosts, the shadows,
Running straight across the heavens,
Filled with spirits and shadows from the past.
At the door on summer evenings
Sat the little Hiawatha;
Heard the whispering of the pine trees,
Heard the gentle lapping of the waters,
Sounds of music, words of wonder;
"Minne-wawa!" said the Pine-trees,
"Mudway-aushka!" said the water.
Saw the firefly, Wah-wah-taysee,
Darting through the twilight of evening,
With the flickering of its candle
Illuminating the brakes and bushes,
And he sang the song of children,
Sang the song Nokomis taught him:
"Wah-wah-taysee, little firefly,"
Little, fluttering, white-fire insect,
Little, dancing, white-fire creature,
Light me with your little candle,
Before I lie down upon my bed,

"Before I close my eyelids in sleep!"
Saw the moon rise from the water
Rippling, rounding from the water,
Saw the flecks and shadows on it,
"What is that, Nokomis?" she whispered.
And good Nokomis answered:
"Once a warrior, very angry,
Grabbed his grandmother and hurled her
Up into the sky at midnight;
Right at the moon he hurled her;
"It's her body that you see there."
Saw the rainbow in the sky,
In the eastern sky, the rainbow,
"What is that, Nokomis?" she whispered.
And good Nokomis answered:
"'It is the heaven of flowers you see there;
All the wildflowers of the forest,
All the lilies of the prairie,
When they fade and die on earth,
"Blossom in that heaven above us."
When he heard the owls at midnight,
Hooting, laughing in the forest,
"What is that?" he cried in terror,
"What is that," he said, "Nokomis?"
And good Nokomis answered:
"That is just the owl and owlet,"
Talking in their native language,
"Talking, scolding at each other."
Then the little Hiawatha
Learned the language of every bird,
Learned their names and all their secrets,
How they built their nests in summer,
Where they concealed themselves during winter,

Talked with them whenever he met them,
Called them "Hiawatha's Chickens."
Of all animals, he mastered their languages.
Learned their names and all their secrets,
How beavers construct their lodges,
Where the squirrels hid their acorns,
How the reindeer ran so swiftly,
Why the rabbit was so fearful,
Talked with them whenever he met them,
Called them "Hiawatha's Brothers."
Then Iagoo, the great boaster,
He was a marvelous storyteller,
He was both the traveler and the storyteller,
He was the friend of old Nokomis,
Made a bow for Hiawatha;
From a branch of ash he made it,
From an oak branch, they crafted the arrows,
Tipped with flint and winged with feathers,
And he made the cord from deer skin.
Then he said to Hiawatha:
"Go, my son, into the forest,"
Where the red deer gather in herds,
Kill a famous roebuck for us,
"Kill a deer with antlers for us!"
Straight ahead into the forest
All alone walked Hiawatha
Proudly, with his bow and arrows;
And the birds sang all around him, above him,
"Don't shoot us, Hiawatha!"
Sang the robin, the Opechee,
Sang the bluebird, the Owaissa,
"Don't shoot us, Hiawatha!"
Up the oak tree, right next to him,

The squirrel Adjidaumo sprang,
In and out among the branches,
Coughed and chattered from the oak tree,
Laughed, and said between his laughing,
"Don't shoot me, Hiawatha!"
And the rabbit from his pathway
Jumped to the side, and from far away
Sitting upright on his hind legs,
Half in fear and half in playfulness,
Saying to the little hunter,
"Don't shoot me, Hiawatha!"
But he paid no attention to them
and didn't hear what they were saying,
For his thoughts were focused on the red deer;
On their tracks his eyes were fixed,
Leading down to the river,
To the ford across the river,
And he walked as if he were sleepwalking.
Hidden in the alder bushes,
There he waited until the deer arrived.
Until he spotted two antlers rising,
Saw two eyes looking from the thicket,
Saw two nostrils pointing toward the wind,
A deer walked down the path.
Dappled with leafy light and shadow.
And his heart fluttered inside him,
Trembled like the leaves above him,
Like the birch leaf trembled,
As the deer walked down the path.
Then, rising up on one knee,
Hiawatha aimed an arrow;
Barely a branch stirred as he moved.
Barely a leaf moved or rustled,

But the cautious deer suddenly jumped back in alarm,
Stamped with all his hooves together,
Listened with one foot raised,
Jumped as if to meet the arrow;
Ah! the singing, deadly arrow,
Like a wasp, it buzzed around him and delivered its sting!
Dead he lay there in the forest,
By the shallow crossing over the river;
Beat his timid heart no longer,
But the heart of Hiawatha
Pulsed and cried out and rejoiced,
As he carried the red deer back home,
And Iagoo and Nokomis
Welcomed his arrival with enthusiastic applause.
From the hide of the red deer, Nokomis
Made a cloak for Hiawatha,
From the red deer's flesh Nokomis
Made a banquet in his honor.
All the villagers came and celebrated with a feast.
All the guests praised Hiawatha,
Called him Strong-Heart, Soan-ge-taha!
Called him Loon-Heart, Mahn-go-taysee!

Chapter IV:
Hiawatha and Mudjekeewis

Out of childhood into manhood
Now Hiawatha had grown up,
Skilled in all the craft of hunters,
Educated in all the ancient wisdom of our elders,
In all youthful sports and pastimes,

In all manly arts and labors.
Swift on his feet was Hiawatha;
He could shoot an arrow away from himself.
And rush ahead with incredible speed,
That the arrow fell behind him!
Strong-armed was Hiawatha;
He could shoot ten arrows upward,
Fire them with such power and speed,
That the tenth arrow had left the bowstring
Before the first one had fallen to earth!
He wore mittens, Minjekahwun,
Magic mittens made of deer-skin;
When he wore them on his hands,
He could strike the rocks apart,
He could crush them into powder.
He had magical moccasins,
Magic moccasins made of deer-skin;
When he wrapped them around his ankles,
When he fastened them to his feet,
At every step, he covered a mile!
Much he questioned old Nokomis
Of his father Mudjekeewis;
Learned from her the fatal secret
Of the beauty of his mother,
Of his father's dishonesty;
And his heart burned with passion inside him,
Like a burning coal, his heart blazed with life.
Then he spoke to old Nokomis,
"I will go to Mudjekeewis,"
See how my father is doing,
At the doorways of the West-Wind,
"At the gates of the Sunset!"
From his lodge, Hiawatha departed,

Dressed for travel, armed for hunting;
Wearing a deerskin shirt and leggings,
Beautifully crafted with feathers and shell beads;
On his head he wore his eagle feathers,
Around his waist he wore his belt of wampum,
In his hand he held his bow made of ash wood,
Strung with reindeer sinews;
In his quiver were oak arrows,
Tipped with jasper, winged with feathers;
With his mittens, Minjekahwun,
With his moccasins enchanted.
Warning said the old Nokomis,
"Do not go forth, O Hiawatha!"
To the kingdom of the West-Wind,
To the lands of Mudjekeewis,
Lest he harm you with his magic,
"Don't let him kill you with his cunning!"
But the fearless Hiawatha
Ignored her woman's warning;
He walked forward into the forest.
At every step, he covered a mile;
The sky above him appeared ghastly and threatening.
The earth below him appeared ghastly and disturbing.
The air around him was hot and stifling,
Filled with smoke and fiery vapors,
As burning woods and prairies,
For his heart burned with passion inside him,
Like a burning coal, his heart blazed with life.
So he traveled westward, westward,
Left the fastest deer behind him,
Left the antelope and bison;
Crossed the rushing Esconaba,
Crossed the mighty Mississippi,

Crossed the Prairie Mountains,
Passed through the land of Crows and Foxes,
Passed the homes of the Blackfeet,
Reached the Rocky Mountains,
To the kingdom of the West-Wind,
Where upon the windy peaks
Sat the ancient Mudjekeewis,
Ruler of the winds of heaven.
Hiawatha was filled with awe
At the sight of his father.
On the air around him wildly
His cloudy hair flowed and swayed in the wind,
His hair gleamed like drifting snow,
Blazed like Ishkoodah, the comet,
Like the star with blazing hair.
Mudjekeewis was filled with joy
When he looked at Hiawatha,
Saw his youth rise up before him
In the face of Hiawatha,
Saw the beauty of Wenonah
From the grave rise up before him.
"Welcome!" he said, "Hiawatha,
To the kingdom of the West-Wind
Long have I been waiting for you
Youth is beautiful, old age is solitary,
Youth burns with passion, while old age grows cold and distant.
You bring back the days that have passed,
You bring back my passionate youth,
"And the beautiful Wenonah!"
Many days they spent talking together,
Questioned, listened, waited, answered;
Much the mighty Mudjekeewis
Bragged about his past achievements,

Of his dangerous adventures,
His unwavering courage,
His invulnerable body.
Hiawatha sat patiently,
Listening to his father's boasting;
With a smile, he sat down and listened.
Spoke neither threat nor warning,
Neither his words nor his expression gave him away.
But his heart burned with passion inside him,
Like a burning coal, his heart blazed with life.
Then he said, "O Mudjekeewis,
Is there nothing that can harm you?
"Nothing that you are afraid of?"
And the mighty Mudjekeewis,
Grand and gracious in his boasting,
Answered, saying, "There is nothing,
Nothing but the black rock over there,
"Nothing but the deadly Wawbeek!"
And he looked at Hiawatha
With a wise expression and kindly demeanor,
With a fatherly expression,
Gazed with pride at the beauty
Of his tall and graceful figure,
"O my Hiawatha!"
Is there anything that can harm you?
"Is there anything you're afraid of?"
But the cautious Hiawatha
Paused for a moment, as if unsure,
Remained silent, as if making a decision,
And then he answered, "There is nothing."
Nothing but the bulrush over there,
"Nothing but the great Apukwa!"
And as Mudjekeewis rose,

He reached out his hand to pick the bulrush,
Hiawatha cried out in terror,
Cried out in carefully disguised terror,
"Kago! kago! do not touch it!"
"Ah, kaween!" said Mudjekeewis,
"No indeed, I will not touch it!"
Then they discussed other topics;
First of Hiawatha's brothers,
First of Wabun, of the East-Wind,
Of the South Wind, Shawondasee,
Of the North, Kabibonokka;
Then of Hiawatha's mother,
Of the beautiful Wenonah,
Of her birth upon the meadow,
Of her death, as old Nokomis
Had remembered and related.
"O Mudjekeewis," he cried out.
It was you who killed Wenonah,
Took her young life and her beauty,
Broke the Lily of the Prairie,
Crushed it under your feet;
"You admit it! You admit it!"
And the mighty Mudjekeewis
Tossed upon the wind his hair,
He bowed his gray head in deep sorrow,
With a quiet nod, he agreed.
Then Hiawatha jumped up,
And with a threatening look and gesture
Laid his hand upon the black rock,
On the deadly Wawbeek he placed it,
With his mittens, Minjekahwun,
Tear the protruding cliff apart,
Struck and shattered it into pieces,

Threw them wildly at his father,
The regretful Mudjekeewis,
For his heart burned with passion inside him,
Like a burning coal, his heart blazed with life.
But the ruler of the West Wind
Blew the fragments backward from him,
With each breath from his nostrils,
With the storm of his rage,
Blew them back at his attacker;
Grabbed the cattail, the Apukwa,
Pulled it out completely with all its roots and fibers
From the edge of the meadow,
From its muddy depths the towering bulrush emerges;
Long and loud laughed Hiawatha!
Then the deadly conflict began.
Hand to hand among the mountains;
From his high perch, the eagle screamed,
The Keneu, the great war-eagle,
Sat on the rocky cliffs surrounding them,
Wheeling flapped his wings above them.
Like a towering tree weathering the storm
The massive bulrush was bent and whipped by the wind;
And in enormous, weighty masses
The deadly Wawbeek came crashing down;
Until the ground trembled from the chaos
And the chaos of the battle,
And the air was filled with shouting.
And the thunder of the mountains,
Starting answered, "Baim-wawa!"
Back retreated Mudjekeewis,
Rushing westward over the mountains,
Stumbling westward down the mountains,
Three entire days they fought while retreating,

Still pursued by Hiawatha
To the doorways of the West-Wind,
To the gates of the Sunset,
To the farthest edges of the earth,
Where into the empty spaces
The sun sets like a flamingo
Settles into her nest when darkness falls
In the gloomy swamplands.
"Stop!" Mudjekeewis finally shouted,
"Wait, my son, my Hiawatha!"
It's impossible to kill me.
For you cannot kill the immortal
I have put you to this test.
But to understand and demonstrate your bravery;
Now receive the prize of valor!
"Go back to your home and people,"
Live among them, work among them,
Cleanse the earth from all that harms it,
Clear the fishing areas and rivers,
Defeat all monsters and magicians,
All the Wendigoes, the giants,
All the serpents, the Kenabeeks,
As I killed the Great Bear,
Killed the Great Bear of the mountains.
"And finally when Death approaches you,"
When the terrible eyes of Pauguk
Glare upon you in the darkness,
I will share my kingdom with you,
You shall be a ruler from now on
Of the Northwest Wind, Keewaydin,
"Of the home-wind, the Keewaydin."
Thus was fought that famous battle
In the terrible days of Shah-shah,

In the days that have long since passed,
In the kingdom of the West Wind.
Still the hunter sees its traces
Scattered far across hill and valley;
Sees the giant bulrush growing
By the ponds and waterways,
Observes the crowds at the Wawbeek
Lying motionless in every valley.
Hiawatha now headed home;
Pleasant was the landscape around him,
Pleasant was the air above him,
For the bitterness of anger
Had completely left him,
From his mind came thoughts of revenge,
From his heart the burning fever.
Only once did he slow his pace,
Only once did he pause or stop,
Stopped to buy arrowheads
Of the ancient Arrow-maker,
In the land of the Dakotas,
Where the Falls of Minnehaha
Flash and gleam among the oak trees,
Laugh and leap into the valley.
There the ancient Arrow-maker
Made his arrow-heads of sandstone,
Arrow-heads of chalcedony,
Arrow-heads of flint and jasper,
Smoothed and sharpened at the edges,
Hard and polished, sharp and valuable.
With him lived his dark-eyed daughter,
Unpredictable as the Minnehaha,
With her shifting moods of darkness and light,
Eyes that alternately smiled and frowned,

Feet as swift as the flowing river,
Tresses flowing like the water,
And as musical a laughter:
And he gave her a name that came from the river,
From the waterfall he gave her a name,
Minnehaha, Laughing Water.
Was it then for arrowheads,
Arrow-heads of chalcedony,
Arrow-heads of flint and jasper,
That my Hiawatha stopped
In the land of the Dakotas?
Was it not to see the maiden,
See the face of Laughing Water
Looking out from behind the curtain,
Hear the rustling of her garments
From behind the flowing curtain,
As one observes the Minnehaha
Shining brightly, flickering through the tree branches,
As one hears the Laughing Water
From behind its screen of branches?
Who can say what thoughts and visions
Fill the passionate minds of young men?
Who can say what beautiful dreams
Filled the heart of Hiawatha?
All of this he shared with old Nokomis,
When he arrived at the lodge as the sun was setting,
Was the meeting with his father,
Was his battle with Mudjekeewis;
Not a single word did he speak about arrows,
Not a single word about Laughing Water.

———————

Chapter V:
Hiawatha's Fasting

You will hear how Hiawatha
Prayed and fasted in the forest,
Not for becoming better at hunting,
Not for becoming more skilled at fishing,
Not for victories in battle,
And fame among the fighters,
But for the benefit of the people,
For the benefit of the nations.
First, he constructed a lodge for fasting.
Built a wigwam in the forest,
By the gleaming Great Water,
In the cheerful and delightful springtime,
In the Moon of Leaves he built it,
And, with many dreams and visions,
Seven complete days and nights he went without food.
On the first day of his fasting
Through the leafy woods he wandered;
Watched the deer leap from the dense brush.
Saw the rabbit in his burrow,
Heard the pheasant, Bena, drumming,
Heard the squirrel, Adjidaumo,
Shaking among his collection of acorns,
Saw the pigeon, the Omeme,
Building nests among the pine trees,
And in flocks the wild goose, Wawa,
Flying to the marshlands northward,
Whirring, wailing far above him.
"Master of Life!" he cried out in despair,
"Must our lives depend on these things?"

On the following day of his fasting
By the river's edge he wandered,
Through the Muskoday, the meadow,
Saw the wild rice, Mahnomonee,
Saw the blueberry, Meenahga,
And the strawberry, Odahmin,
And the gooseberry, Shahbomin,
And the grapevine, the Bemahgut,
Drifting over the alder branches,
Filling all the air with fragrance!
"Master of Life!" he cried out in despair,
"Must our lives depend on these things?"
On the third day of his fasting
By the lake he sat and thought deeply.
By the calm, clear water;
Saw the sturgeon, Nahma, leaping,
Scattering drops like beads of wampum,
Saw the yellow perch, the Sahwa,
Like a ray of sunlight in the water,
Saw the pike, the Maskenozha,
And the herring, Okahahwis,
And the Shawgashee, the crawfish!
"Master of Life!" he cried out in despair,
"Must our lives depend on these things?"
On the fourth day of his fasting
In his lodge he lay exhausted;
From his bed of leaves and branches
Gazing with half-open eyelids,
Full of shadowy dreams and visions,
On the dizzying, swirling landscape,
On the shimmering of the water,
On the splendor of the sunset.
And he saw a young man approaching,

Dressed in garments green and yellow,
Coming through the purple twilight,
Through the splendor of the sunset;
Feathers of green curved over his forehead,
And his hair was soft and golden.
Standing at the open doorway,
Long he gazed at Hiawatha,
Viewed with sympathy and understanding
On his wasted body and face,
And, in tones that sounded like sighing
Of the South Wind in the treetops,
"O my Hiawatha!" he said.
All your prayers are heard in heaven,
For you don't pray like the others;
Not for becoming better at hunting,
Not for becoming more skilled at fishing,
Not for victory in battle,
Nor fame among the fighters,
But for the benefit of the people,
For the benefit of the nations.
"From the Master of Life descending,
I, the friend of humanity, Mondamin,
Come to warn you and teach you,
How through struggle and hard work
You will receive what you have prayed for.
Rise up from your bed of branches,
"Get up, young person, and fight me!"
Weak from hunger, Hiawatha
Started from his bed of branches,
From the dim light of his tepee
Forth into the flush of sunset
Came, and wrestled with Mondamin;
At his touch, he felt renewed courage.

Pulsing through his mind and chest,
Felt renewed life, hope, and energy
Run through every nerve and fiber.
So they wrestled there together
In the glory of the sunset,
And the harder they fought and struggled,
Hiawatha grew even stronger;
Until the darkness surrounded them,
And the heron, the Shuh-shuh-gah,
From her nest nestled among the pine trees,
Gave a cry of lamentation,
Gave a scream of pain and hunger.
"That's enough!" said Mondamin then,
Smiling upon Hiawatha,
"But tomorrow, when the sun sets,
"I will come again to test you."
And he disappeared and was never seen again;
Whether falling like the rain falls,
Whether rising like mist rises,
Hiawatha didn't see, didn't know,
Only saw that he had disappeared,
Leaving him alone and unconscious,
With the foggy lake beneath him,
And the spinning stars above him.
On the following day and the day after that,
When the sun descends through the heavens,
Like a red and burning ember
From the heart of the Great Spirit,
Fell into the western waters,
Mondamin came for the trial,
For the conflict with Hiawatha;
Arrived as quietly as the morning dew settles,
From the empty air appearing,

Into empty air returning,
Taking form when it makes contact with the earth,
But invisible to everyone
In its arrival and departure.
Three times they wrestled there together
In the glory of the sunset,
Until the darkness surrounded them,
Until the heron, the Shuh-shuh-gah,
From her nest nestled among the pine trees,
Cried out loudly from hunger,
And Mondamin stopped to listen.
Tall and beautiful he stood there,
In his clothes of green and yellow;
To and fro his feathers above him,
Waved and nodded with his breathing,
And the sweat of the encounter
Clung to him like dewdrops.
"O Hiawatha!" he cried out.
Bravely have you wrestled with me,
Three times you have wrestled fiercely with me,
And the Master of Life, who sees us,
"He will give you the victory!"
Then he smiled and said: "Tomorrow"
Is the final day of your struggle,
Is the last day of your fasting.
You will conquer and overcome me;
Make a bed for me to lie in,
Where the rain may fall upon me,
Where the sun can come and warm me;
Strip off these clothes, green and yellow,
Remove this drooping feathers from me,
Lay me in the earth, and make it
Soft and loose and light above me.

"Let no hand disturb my slumber,"
Let no weed or worm bother me,
Let not Kahgahgee, the raven,
Come to haunt me and torment me,
Only come yourself to watch me,
Until I awaken, and begin, and come alive,
"Until I leap into the sunshine"
And with those words, he left;
Hiawatha slept peacefully,
But he heard the Wawonaissa,
Heard the whippoorwill complaining,
Sitting on top of his solitary tent;
Heard the rushing Sebowisha,
Heard the small stream flowing gently beside him,
Talking to the darksome forest;
Heard the sighing of the branches,
As they rose and fell
At the passing of the night wind,
Heard them, as one hears in sleep
Far-off murmurs, dreamy whispers:
Hiawatha slept peacefully.
On the following day, Nokomis arrived,
On the seventh day of his fasting,
Brought food for Hiawatha,
Came begging and lamenting,
So that his hunger wouldn't overcome him,
Lest his fasting should prove deadly.
But he neither tasted nor touched anything.
"Nokomis," he said to her,
Wait until the sun is setting,
Until the darkness surrounds us,
Until the heron, the Shuh-shuh-gah,
Crying from the desolate marshes,

"Tells us that the day is ended."
Nokomis went home weeping,
Grieving for her beloved Hiawatha,
Worried that his strength might give out,
Lest his fasting should be fatal.
He sat there exhausted, waiting in the meantime.
For the arrival of Mondamin,
Until the shadows point eastward,
Stretched across field and forest,
Until the sun fell from the sky,
Drifting on the waters toward the west,
As a red leaf in the autumn
Falls and floats upon the water,
Falls and sinks into its embrace.
And look! the young Mondamin,
With his soft and gleaming hair,
With his clothes in green and yellow,
With his long and shiny feathers,
Stood and beckoned at the doorway.
And like someone walking in their sleep,
Pale and exhausted, but fearless,
From the wigwam Hiawatha
Came and wrestled with Mondamin.
Around him, the landscape spun in circles.
Sky and forest spun together,
And his powerful heart pounded inside his chest,
As the sturgeon jumps and fights
In a net to break its meshes.
Like a ring of fire around him
The red horizon blazed and flared with brilliant light.
And a hundred suns seemed to be watching
At the wrestling match.
Suddenly on the grass

All alone stood Hiawatha,
Breathing heavily from his frantic effort,
Trembling with the fight;
And before him breathless, lifeless,
Place the young man, with his hair in disarray,
Feathers ripped and clothes in shreds,
Dead he lay there in the sunset.
And victorious Hiawatha
Made the grave exactly as he had ordered.
Stripped the clothes from Mondamin,
Tore away his worn and ragged feathers,
Buried him in the ground, and created it
Soft and loose and light above him;
And the heron, the Shuh-shuh-gah,
From the gloomy moorlands,
Gave a cry of lamentation,
Cried out in pain and anguish!
Hiawatha then headed home
To the lodge of old Nokomis,
And the seven days of his fasting
Were accomplished and completed.
But the place was not forgotten
Where he fought with Mondamin;
Nor forgotten nor neglected
Was the grave where Mondamin lay,
Sleeping in the rain and sunshine,
Where his scattered feathers and clothing lay
Faded in the rain and sunshine.
Day after day, Hiawatha
Go and wait beside it, keeping watch;
Kept the dark soil soft above it,
Kept it free from weeds and insects,
Drove away, with scoffs and shoutings,

Kahgahgee, the king of ravens.
Until finally a small green feather
From the ground, something rose slowly upward,
Then another and another,
And before the summer ended
The corn stood in all its beauty,
With its gleaming garments surrounding it,
And its long, soft, yellow hair;
And in rapture Hiawatha
Cried out loudly, "It is Mondamin!"
"Yes, the friend of humanity, Mondamin!"
Then he called out to old Nokomis
And Iagoo, the great boaster,
Showed them where the corn was growing,
Told them of his wondrous vision,
Of his struggle and his victory,
Of this new gift to the nations,
Which should be their food forever.
And even later, when autumn arrived
Changed the long, green leaves to yellow,
And the soft and juicy kernels
Grew like wampum hard and yellow,
Then he collected the ripe grain.
Removed the dried, dead outer coverings from them,
As he had once stripped the wrestler,
Hosted the first Feast of Mondamin,
And made it known to the people
This new gift from the Great Spirit.

———————

Chapter VI:
Hiawatha's Friends

Two close friends belonged to Hiawatha,
Chosen from among all the rest,
Bound to him in the closest union,
And to whom he extended his right hand
Of his heart, in joy and sorrow;
Chibiabos, the musician,
And the incredibly strong man, Kwasind.
Straight between them ran the pathway,
Never did grass grow upon it;
Singing birds that speak lies,
Story-tellers, troublemakers,
Found no one willing to listen,
Could not create hostility between them,
For they kept each other's secrets,
Spoke with naked hearts together,
Thinking deeply and planning extensively
How human communities might flourish.
Most beloved by Hiawatha
Was the gentle Chibiabos,
He was the greatest of all musicians,
He was the sweetest of all singers.
Beautiful and childlike was he,
Brave as a man is, gentle as a woman,
Flexible as a willow branch,
Majestic as a deer with antlers.
When he sang, the village listened;
All the warriors gathered around him,
All the women came to listen to him;
Now he ignited their hearts with intense emotion,

Now he moved them to compassion.
From the hollow reeds he created
Flutes so musical and mellow,
That the brook, the Sebowisha,
The murmuring in the woodland stopped,
That the forest birds stopped their singing,
And the squirrel, Adjidaumo,
The chattering in the oak tree stopped.
And the rabbit, the Wabasso,
Sat up straight to observe and pay attention.
Yes, the brook, the Sebowisha,
Pausing, he said, "O Chibiabos,
Teach my waves to flow in music,
"Softly as your words in singing!"
Yes, the bluebird, the Owaissa,
"O Chibiabos," said Envious,
Teach me melodies as untamed and unpredictable,
"Teach me songs filled with wild passion!"
Yes, the robin, the Opechee,
Joyous, said, "O Chibiabos,
Teach me melodies that are sweet and gentle,
"Teach me songs filled with joy!"
And the whippoorwill, Wawonaissa,
Sobbing, said, "O Chibiabos,
Teach me tones as melancholy,
"Teach me songs filled with sorrow!"
All the countless sounds found in nature
Borrowed sweetness from his singing;
All human hearts were softened
By the emotional power of his music;
For he sang of peace and freedom,
Sang of beauty, love, and longing;
Sang of death, and life undying

In the Islands of the Blessed,
In the kingdom of Ponemah,
In the land of the Hereafter.
Very dear to Hiawatha
Was the gentle Chibiabos,
He was the greatest of all musicians,
He was the sweetest of all singers;
For his kindness, he loved him,
And the magic of his singing.
Dear, too, to Hiawatha
Was the incredibly strong man, Kwasind,
He was the strongest of all mortals,
He was the most powerful among many;
For his very strength he loved him,
For his strength combined with goodness.
Kwasind was lazy during his youth,
Very listless, dull, and dreamy,
Never played with other children,
Never fished and never hunted,
Not like other children was he;
But they noticed that he fasted frequently.
Much his spirit guide pleaded,
Much besought his Guardian Spirit.
"Lazy Kwasind!" said his mother,
"You never help me with my work!"
In the summer you are wandering
Wandering aimlessly through the fields and forests;
In the winter you are huddled up
Over the firebrands in the wigwam!
In the coldest days of winter
I need to break through the ice to go fishing;
With my nets you never help me!
At the door my nets are hanging,

Soaking wet and freezing from the water;
Go and wring them, Yenadizze!
"Go and dry them in the sunshine!"
Slowly, from the ashes, Kwasind
Rose, but didn't respond with anger;
From the lodge, they departed in silence,
Took the nets that were tangled together,
Soaking wet and shivering at the entrance;
Like a wisp of straw he twisted them,
Like a wisp of straw he broke them,
Could not twist them without breaking,
Such was the strength in his fingers.
"Lazy Kwasind!" said his father,
"You never help me when I'm hunting;"
Every bow you touch is broken,
Every arrow was broken in half;
Yet come with me to the forest,
"You shall bring the hunting homeward."
Down a narrow pass they wandered,
Where a small stream guided them forward,
Where the paths of deer and buffalo cross
Noticed the soft mud along the edge,
Until they discovered that all further passage was blocked
Shut against them, barred securely
By the trunks of trees that have been uprooted,
Lying lengthwise, lying crosswise,
And blocking any further passage.
"We have to go back," the old man said.
"We cannot climb over these logs;"
Not a single groundhog could make it through them,
"Not a single squirrel can climb over them!"
And immediately he lit his pipe,
And sat down to smoke and think things over.

But before he finished smoking his pipe,
Look! The path was cleared before him;
All the logs had been lifted by Kwasind,
To the right, to the left,
Shot the pine trees swift as arrows,
Threw the cedar trees around like they were lightweight spears.
"Lazy Kwasind!" said the young men,
As they played in the meadow:
"Why are you standing there just staring at us,
Leaning on the rock behind you?
Come and wrestle with the others,
"Let's throw the ring together!"
Lazy Kwasind made no answer,
To their challenge, he made no answer.
Only rose, and slowly turning,
Gripped the massive stone with his hands,
Ripped it from its deep foundation,
Held it suspended in the air for a moment,
Threw it straight down into the river,
Straight down into the rushing Pauwating,
Where it can still be observed during the summer months.
Once as down that foaming river,
Down the rapids of Pauwating,
Kwasind sailed with his companions,
In the stream he saw a beaver,
Saw Ahmeek, the King of Beavers,
Battling against the swift-moving waters,
Rising, sinking in the water.
Without saying a word, without stopping,
Kwasind jumped into the river,
Submerged below the churning surface,
Through the swirling waters, the beaver was pursued,
Followed him among the islands,

Remained underwater for such a long time,
That his terrified companions
"Alas! Farewell to Kwasind!" they cried.
"We will never see Kwasind again!"
But he came back victorious,
And upon his shining shoulders
Brought the beaver, dead and dripping,
Brought the King of all the Beavers.
And these two, as I have told you,
Were the friends of Hiawatha,
Chibiabos, the musician,
And the incredibly strong man, Kwasind.
Long they lived in peace together,
Spoke with naked hearts together,
Thinking deeply and planning extensively
How human communities might thrive.

———————

Chapter VII:
Hiawatha's Sailing

"Give me some of your bark, O Birch tree!"
Of your yellow bark, O Birch tree!
Growing by the rushing river,
Tall and majestic in the valley!
I will build myself a light canoe,
Build a fast canoe for sailing,
That will drift along the river,
Like a yellow leaf in autumn,
Like a yellow water-lily!
"Take off your cloak, O Birch-tree!"
Set aside your pale covering,

For the summertime is coming,
And the sun shines warmly in heaven,
"And you don't need any white-skin wrapper!"
Thus Hiawatha cried out loud
In the lonely forest,
By the rushing Taquamenaw,
When the birds were singing cheerfully,
In the Moon of Leaves were singing,
And the sun, awakening from sleep,
Started up and said, "Look at me!"
"Gheezis, the great Sun, behold me!"
And the tree with all its branches
Rustled in the morning breeze,
Saying, with a sigh of patience,
"Take my cloak, O Hiawatha!"
With his knife he cut around the tree;
Just beneath its lowest branches,
Just above the roots, he cut it,
Until the sap began flowing outward;
Down the trunk, from top to bottom,
He split the bark completely apart,
With a wooden wedge he lifted it,
Removed it from the trunk in one piece.
"Give me some of your branches, O Cedar!"
Of your strong and flexible branches,
My canoe to make more steady,
"Make me stronger and more steadfast!"
Through the summit of the Cedar
A sound rang out, a cry of horror,
A murmur of resistance arose;
But it whispered, leaning down,
"Take my branches, O Hiawatha!"
Down he chopped the cedar branches,

Immediately shaped them into a framework,
Like two bows, he formed and shaped them,
Like two curved bows joined together.
"Give me some of your roots, O Tamarack!"
Of your fibrous roots, O Larch-tree!
My canoe to bind together,
So to tie the ends together
That the water may not enter,
"So the river won't get me wet!"
And the Larch, with all its fibers,
Trembled in the morning air,
Touched his forehead with its tassels,
Slipped away with one long, sorrowful sigh.
"Take them all, O Hiawatha!"
From the earth he pulled the fibers,
Tore apart the strong roots of the Larch tree,
Carefully stitched the bark together,
Secure it tightly to the framework.
"Give me some of your healing balm, O Fir-tree!"
Of your healing balm and your resin,
So to close the seams together
That the water may not enter,
"So the river won't get me wet!"
And the Fir-tree, tall and dark,
Wept through all its layers of darkness,
Shaken like a coastline covered with stones,
Responded with wailing, responded with weeping,
"Take my balm, O Hiawatha!"
And he took the tears of balsam,
Took the resin of the fir tree,
Spread across every crack and opening,
Made every crack secure from water.
"Give me some of your quills, O Hedgehog!"

All your quills, O Kagh, the Hedgehog!
I will make a necklace of them,
Make a belt for my beloved,
"And two stars to adorn her chest!"
From a hollow tree the Hedgehog
With his drowsy eyes, he looked at him.
Shot his gleaming quills, like arrows,
Saying with a sleepy murmur,
Through the mess of his whiskers,
"Take my quills, O Hiawatha!"
From the ground he collected the quills,
All the little shining arrows,
Stained them red and blue and yellow,
With the juice of roots and berries;
Into his canoe he crafted them,
Around its waist was a gleaming belt,
Around its front, a shining necklace,
On its chest, two brilliant stars shine.
Thus the birch canoe was built.
In the valley, by the river,
In the heart of the forest;
And the life of the forest was within it,
All its mystery and its magic,
All the lightness of the birch tree,
All the strength of the cedar,
All the flexible strength of the larch tree;
And it floated on the river
Like a yellow leaf in autumn,
Like a yellow water lily.
Hiawatha had no paddles,
He had no paddles and didn't need any,
For his thoughts served as paddles for him,
And his desires helped direct his path;

Swift or slow, he moved at will through the water,
Turned to the right or left whenever they wanted.
Then he called out loudly to Kwasind,
To his friend, the strong man, Kwasind,
Saying, "Help me clear this river"
"Of its sunken logs and sand-bars."
Straight into the river Kwasind
Dove down like an otter,
Dove down like a beaver,
Stood up to his waist in water,
To his armpits in the river,
Swam and explored in the river,
Pulled at submerged logs and branches,
With his hands he scooped up the sandbars,
With his feet in the mud and tangled weeds.
And so my Hiawatha set sail
Down the rushing Taquamenaw,
Navigated through all its curves and twists,
Sailed through all its depths and shallow waters,
While his friend, the powerful man, Kwasind,
Swam through the deep waters and waded
through the shallow ones.
Up and down the river they went,
In and out among its islands,
Cleared its bed of roots and sandbars,
Pulled the dead trees from its waterway,
Made its journey safe and secure,
Made a pathway for the people,
From its origins in the mountains,
To the waters of Pauwating,
To the bay of Taquamenaw.

––––––––––

Chapter VIII:
Hiawatha's Fishing

Forth upon Lake Superior,
On the sparkling Great Lake,
With his fishing line made of cedar,
Of the twisted bark of cedar,
Forth to catch the sturgeon Nahma,
Mishe-Nahma, King of Fishes,
In his birch canoe rejoicing
All alone went Hiawatha.
Through the clear, transparent water
He could see the fish swimming
Far down in the depths below him;
See the yellow perch, the Sahwa,
Like a ray of sunlight in the water,
See the Shawgashee, the crayfish,
Like a spider at the bottom,
On the white and sandy bottom.
At the back of the boat sat Hiawatha,
With his fishing line made of cedar;
In his feathers the morning breeze
Played as in the hemlock branches;
On the front of the ship, with its tail raised high,
Sat the squirrel, Adjidaumo;
In his fur the morning breeze
Played as in the prairie grasses.
On the white sand of the bottom
Lay the monster Mishe-Nahma,
Lay the sturgeon, King of Fishes;
Through his gills he breathed the water,
With his fins he stirred and sifted,

With his tail, he swept the sandy floor.
There he lay in all his armor;
On each side a shield to protect him,
Plates of bone upon his forehead,
Down his sides, back, and shoulders
Bone plates with protruding spines
He was painted with his war paint.
Stripes of yellow, red, and azure,
Patches of brown and patches of black;
And he lay there on the bottom,
Fanning with his purple fins,
As above him Hiawatha
In his birch canoe he came sailing,
With his fishing line made of cedar.
"Take my bait," cried Hiawatha,
Dawn into the depths beneath him,
"Take my bait, O Sturgeon, Nahma!"
Come up from beneath the water,
"Let's see which one is stronger!"
And he cast his cedar fishing line into the water.
Through the clear, transparent water,
Waited in vain for a response,
Long sat waiting for an answer,
And repeating louder and louder,
"Take my bait, O King of Fishes!"
Quietly lay the sturgeon, Nahma,
Gently waving in the water,
Looking up at Hiawatha,
Hearing his call and outcry,
His pointless chaos,
Until he grew tired of the shouting;
And he said to the Kenozha,
To the pike, the Maskenozha,

"Take the bait of this rude fellow,"
"Break the line of Hiawatha!"
In his fingers Hiawatha
Felt the slack line suddenly jolt and pull tight,
As he pulled it in, it tugged so
The birch canoe stood upright on its end.
Like a birch log floating in the water,
With the squirrel, Adjidaumo,
Perched and playfully moving about on the peak.
Full of contempt was Hiawatha
When he saw the fish swimming upward,
Saw the pike, the Maskenozha,
Coming closer, closer to him,
And he shouted through the water,
"Esa! esa! shame upon you!"
You are nothing more than the pike, Kenozha,
You are not the fish I wanted,
"You are not the King of Fishes!"
Spiraling down to the depths
The pike sank in great confusion.
And the mighty sturgeon, Nahma,
Said to Ugudwash, the sunfish,
To the bream, with scales of crimson,
"Take the bait of this great boaster,"
"Break the line of Hiawatha!"
Slowly upward, wavering, gleaming,
Rose the Ugudwash, the sun-fish,
Grabbed Hiawatha's fishing line,
Threw his entire body weight into it,
Made a whirlpool in the water,
The birch canoe spun around in circles,
Round and round in swirling whirlpools,
Until the ripples in the water

Reached the distant sandy shores,
Until the water-flags and rushes
Nodded on the distant margins.
But when Hiawatha saw him
Slowly rising through the water,
Raising his brilliant disk,
Loud he shouted in derision,
"Esa! esa! shame upon you!"
You are Ugudwash, the sun-fish,
You are not the fish I wanted,
"You are not the King of Fishes!"
Slowly downward, wavering, gleaming,
Sank the Ugudwash, the sun-fish,
And once again the sturgeon, Nahma,
Heard the shout of Hiawatha,
Heard his bold challenge of rebellion,
The unnecessary commotion,
Echoing far across the water.
From the white sand of the bottom
Up he stood with an angry gesture,
Trembling in every nerve and fiber,
Clashing all his plates of armor,
Shining brilliantly with all his war paint;
In his anger he shot upward,
Flashing leaped into the sunshine,
Opened his massive jaws and swallowed
Both canoe and Hiawatha.
Down into that dark cavern
Hiawatha plunged headfirst downward,
As a log floating on some dark river
Rushes and plunges down the rapids,
Found himself in complete darkness,
Searched around in helpless confusion,

Until he felt a powerful heart beating,
Pulsing in that complete darkness.
And he struck it in his anger,
With his fist, the heart of Nahma,
Felt the mighty King of Fishes
Shudder through each nerve and fiber,
Heard the water bubble around him
As he jumped and stumbled through it,
Heartbroken, weak, and exhausted.
Hiawatha then crossed over
Drag his birch-bark canoe to safety,
Unless from the jaws of Nahma,
In the chaos and disorder,
He could be thrown forward and die.
And the squirrel, Adjidaumo,
Searched and talked very cheerfully,
Worked and struggled alongside Hiawatha
Until the work was finished.
Then Hiawatha said to him,
"O my little friend, the squirrel,
Bravely have you toiled to help me;
Take Hiawatha's gratitude,
And the name he now gives you;
For the future and for all time
Boys shall call you Adjidaumo,
"Tail-in-air the boys shall call you!"
And once again the sturgeon, Nahma,
Gasped and trembled in the water,
Then everything became still, and drifted toward the shore
Until he scraped against the pebbles,
Until the attentive Hiawatha
Heard him scrape against the shore,
Felt him wash ashore on the pebbles,

Knew that Nahma, King of Fishes,
Lay there dead upon the edge.
Then he heard a clang and flapping,
As if many wings were gathering together,
Heard screaming and chaos.
As birds of prey fight against each other,
Saw a gleam of light above him,
Shining through the ribs of Nahma,
Saw the sparkling eyes of seagulls,
Of Kayoshk, the seagulls, watching,
Gazing at him through the opening,
Heard them saying to each other,
"'It's our brother, Hiawatha!'"
And he called out from beneath them,
Shouted triumphantly from the caves:
"O you seagulls! O my brothers!"
I have killed the sturgeon, Nahma;
Make the gaps a bit wider,
With your claws, the openings grow wider.
Set me free from this dark prison,
And from this point forward and forever
Men will talk about your accomplishments,
Calling you Kayoshk, the sea-gulls,
"Yes, Kayoshk, the Noble Scratchers!"
And the wild and noisy seagulls
Worked hard with both beak and claws,
Made the cracks and gaps larger
In the massive ribs of Nahma,
And from danger and from jail,
From the body of the sturgeon,
From the danger of the water,
They released my Hiawatha.
He was standing near his wigwam,

On the edge of the water,
And he called out to old Nokomis,
Called and beckoned to Nokomis,
Pointed to the sturgeon, Nahma,
Lying lifeless on the pebbles,
With the seagulls feeding on him.
"I have killed the Mishe-Nahma,
"I've killed the King of Fishes!" he said;
"Look! the sea-gulls feed upon him,"
Yes, my friends Kayoshk, the seagulls;
Drive them not away, Nokomis,
They have rescued me from tremendous danger.
In the body of the sturgeon,
Wait until they finish eating.
Until their stomachs are completely filled with feasting,
Until they fly homeward at sunset,
To their nests among the marshes;
Then bring all your pots and kettles,
"And make oil for us in Winter."
And she waited until the sun set,
Until the pale moon, the Night-sun,
Rose above the calm water,
Until Kayoshk, the satisfied seagulls,
From their feast they arose with loud shouting.
And across the fiery sunset
Flew to distant islands,
To their nests among the rushes.
To his sleep went Hiawatha,
And Nokomis went to her work,
Working steadily in the moonlight,
Until the sun and moon switched positions,
Until the sky turned red with sunrise,
And Kayoshk, the hungry seagulls,

Returned from the marshy islands,
Loudly demanding their morning feast.
Three complete days and nights pass in succession
Old Nokomis and the Seagulls
Stripped away the oily flesh of Nahma,
Until the waves flowed through the rib bones,
Until the seagulls stopped coming,
And nothing lay upon the sands
But the skeleton of Nahma.

Chapter IX:
Hiawatha and the Pearl-Feather

On the shores of Gitche Gumee,
Of the sparkling Great Lakes,
Nokomis stood there, the old woman,
Pointing with her finger toward the west,
Over the water pointing westward,
To the purple clouds of sunset.
Fiercely the red sun descending
Blazed his path across the sky,
Set the sky on fire behind him,
As war parties retreat,
Burn the prairies on their war-trail;
And the moon, the Night-sun, eastward,
Suddenly springing from his hiding place,
Quickly followed those bloody footprints,
Followed in that blazing path of war,
With its harsh light shining on his face.
And Nokomis, the old woman,
Pointing with her finger toward the west,

Spoke these words to Hiawatha:
"Over there lives the great Pearl-Feather,"
Megissogwon, the Magician,
Manito of Wealth and Wampum,
Guarded by his fiery serpents,
Guarded by the black pitch-water.
You can see his fiery serpents,
The Kenabeek, the great serpents,
Twisting and turning, frolicking in the water;
You can see the black tar-like water
Extending far into the distance beyond them,
To the purple clouds of sunset!
"He was the one who killed my father,"
By his evil schemes and cleverness,
When he came down from the moon,
When he came to earth to find me.
He, the most powerful of all Magicians,
Sends the fever from the marshes,
Sends the disease-carrying fumes,
Releases toxic vapors,
Sends the white fog from the marshlands,
Brings sickness and death upon us!
"Take your bow, O Hiawatha,"
Take your arrows with jasper tips,
Take your war-club, Puggawaugun,
And your mittens, Minjekahwun,
And your birch canoe for sailing,
And the oil of Mishe-Nahma,
So to coat its sides, that quickly
You may pass through the black tar-like water;
Defeat this ruthless sorcerer,
Save the people from the fever
That he breathes across the marshlands,

"And avenge my father's murder!"
Immediately then my Hiawatha
Armed himself with all his war-gear,
Launched his birch canoe for sailing;
With the palm of his hand, he gently patted its sides.
"Cheemaun, my darling," he said with glee,
O my birch canoe! leap forward,
Where you see the fiery serpents,
"Where you see the black pitch-water!"
Cheemaun leaped forward with joy,
And the noble Hiawatha
Sang his wild and sorrowful war song,
And above him the war-eagle,
The Keneu, the great war-eagle,
Master of all birds with feathers,
Screamed and hurtled through the heavens.
Soon he reached the fiery serpents,
The Kenabeek, the great serpents,
Lying massive on the water,
Sparkling, rippling in the water,
Lying coiled across the passage,
With their fiery crests raised high,
Breathing fiery mists and vapors,
So that no one could go past them.
But the fearless Hiawatha
Cried out loudly, and spoke in this way,
"Let me go on my way, Kenabeek,"
"Let me continue on my journey!"
And they responded, hissing with fierce intensity,
With their fiery breath, they responded:
"Back, go back! O Shaugodaya!"
"Go back to old Nokomis, you coward!"
Then the furious Hiawatha

Raised his powerful bow made of ash wood,
Grabbed his arrows with jasper tips,
Shot them quickly among the snakes;
Every vibration of the bowstring
Was a war-cry and a death-cry,
Every arrow that whistles through the air
Was a death-song of Kenabeek.
Thrashing about in the blood-stained water,
Dead lay all the fiery serpents,
And among them was Hiawatha
Harmless set sail and shouted triumphantly:
"Forward, O Cheemaun, my darling!"
"Onward to the black pitch-water!"
Then he took the oil of Nahma,
And the bows and sides were anointed,
Coated them thoroughly with oil, which quickly
He could cross the dark, tar-like water.
All night long he sailed upon it,
Sailed across those slow-moving waters,
Covered with the dust and decay of countless years,
Black with decaying water reeds,
Adorned with banners and lily petals,
Stagnant, lifeless, dreary, dismal,
Illuminated by the gleaming moonlight,
And illuminated by will-o'-the-wisps,
Fires lit by the spirits of the dead,
In their exhausted nighttime camps.
All the air was white with moonlight,
All the water dark with shadow,
And around him the Suggema,
The mosquito sang his war-song,
And the fireflies, Wah-wah-taysee,
Waved their torches to mislead him;

And the bullfrog, the Dahinda,
Thrust his head into the moonlight,
Fixed his yellow eyes upon him,
Sobbed and sank beneath the surface;
And soon a thousand whistles,
Answered across all the marshlands,
And the heron, the Shuh-shuh-gah,
Far away on the marshy shoreline,
Announced the hero's arrival.
Hiawatha traveled westward in this way,
Toward the realm of Megissogwon,
Toward the land of the Pearl-Feather,
Until the level moon stared at him
His face appeared pale and gaunt.
Until the sun grew hot behind him,
Until it blazed against his shoulders,
And before him on the highland
He could see the Shining Wigwam
Of the Spirit of Wampum,
Of the Most Powerful Magicians.
Then once again he gently patted Cheemaun,
To his birch-bark canoe he said, "Move forward!"
And it stirred in every fiber of its being,
And with one great leap of victory
Jumped across the water lilies,
Jumped through twisted banners and reeds,
And on the beach beyond them
Hiawatha stepped onto dry land without getting his feet wet.
Immediately he picked up his bow made of ash wood,
On the sand he rested one end,
With his knee, he pressed against the center,
Pulled the trusty bowstring taut,
Took an arrow with a jasper head,

Shot it at the Shining Wigwam,
Sent it singing as a herald,
As someone who carries his message,
Of his bold and proud challenge:
"Come out of your lodge, Pearl-Feather!"
"Hiawatha waits your coming!"
Immediately from the Glowing Tepee
Came the mighty Megissogwon,
Tall in height, broad in the shoulders,
Dark and terrifying in appearance,
Dressed from head to toe in wampum,
Armed with all his battle weapons,
Painted like the sky of morning,
Streaked with crimson, blue, and yellow,
Crowned with magnificent eagle feathers,
Flowing upward, flowing outward.
"Well I know you, Hiawatha!"
"Cried he in a voice of thunder,"
In a tone of loud mockery.
"Hurry back, O Shaugodaya!"
Hurry back to the women,
Back to old Nokomis, you coward!
I will kill you where you stand.
"Just as I killed her father long ago!"
But my Hiawatha answered,
Nothing intimidated, afraid of nothing:
"Grand speeches don't strike like weapons of war,"
Bragging words are not a bowstring,
Insults don't cut as deeply as arrows do.
Actions speak louder than words.
"Actions speak louder than boastful words!"
Then the greatest battle began.
That the sun had ever gazed upon,

That the war-birds had ever seen.
All through a summer's day it continued,
From sunrise to sunset;
For the arrows of Hiawatha
The harmless arrow struck the wampum shirt.
The strikes he delivered against it caused no damage.
With his mittens, Minjekahwun,
The heavy war-club fell harmlessly;
It could smash the rocks apart,
But it couldn't break through the net.
Of that magical shirt made of wampum.
Until sunset arrived, Hiawatha,
Leaning on his ash wood bow,
Injured, exhausted, and losing hope,
With his powerful war club shattered,
With his mittens torn and tattered,
And only three useless arrows,
Stopped to rest under a pine tree,
From whose branches the moss hung down,
And whose trunk was covered over
With the leather from the dead man's moccasins,
With the fungus white and yellow.
Suddenly from the branches above him
Sang the Mama, the woodpecker:
"Aim your arrows, Hiawatha,"
At the head of Megissogwon,
Strike the tuft of hair on it,
At the roots of their long black hair;
"That's the only place where he can be hurt!"
Adorned with feathers and crowned with jasper tips,
Swift flew Hiawatha's arrow,
Just as Megissogwon, bending down,
Lifted a heavy stone to hurl it.

Full upon the crown it struck him,
At the base of his long hair,
And he swayed and stumbled forward,
Charging forward like an injured buffalo,
Yes, like Pezhekee, the bison,
When snow covers the prairie.
Swifter flew the second arrow,
In the path of the other,
Cutting deeper than the other,
Causing deeper pain than the other;
And the knees of Megissogwon
Trembled like reeds swaying in the wind beneath him,
Bent and trembled like the rushes.
But the third and most recent arrow
Swiftest flew, and wounded most severely,
And the mighty Megissogwon
Saw the fiery eyes of Pauguk,
Saw the eyes of Death glare at him,
Heard his voice call in the darkness;
At the feet of Hiawatha
Lifeless lay the great Pearl-Feather,
Lay the mightiest of Magicians.
Then the grateful Hiawatha
Called the Mama, the woodpecker,
From his position high up in the tree branches
Of the sorrowful pine tree,
And, in honor of his service,
Stained with blood, the tuft of feathers
On the little head of Mama;
Even to this day he wears it,
Wears the tuft of crimson feathers,
As a symbol of his service.
Then he removed the shirt made of wampum

From the back of Megissogwon,
As a trophy of the battle,
As a symbol of his victory.
On the shore he left the body,
Half on land and half in water,
In the sand, his feet were buried.
And his face was in the water.
And above him, circled and cried out
The Keneu, the great war-eagle,
Sailing around in tighter circles,
Hovering nearer, nearer, nearer.
From the wigwam Hiawatha
Carried the riches of Megissogwon,
All his riches of animal pelts and shell beads,
Furs of bison and of beaver,
Furs of sable and of ermine,
Wampum belts and strings and pouches,
Quivers decorated with beads of wampum,
Filled with arrows that have silver tips.
Then he sailed home in triumph,
Heading home through the dark, tar-black water,
Heading home through the churning serpents,
With the spoils of war,
With a shout and song of triumph.
On the shore stood old Nokomis,
On the shore stood Chibiabos,
And Kwasind, the incredibly strong man,
Waiting for the hero's arrival,
Listening to his songs of triumph.
And the people of the village
Welcomed him with songs and dances,
Made a joyous feast, and shouted:
"Honor be to Hiawatha!"

He has killed the great Pearl-Feather,
Killed the most powerful of Magicians,
Him, who sent the burning fever,
Sent the white fog from the marshlands,
"Sent disease and death among us!"
Ever dear to Hiawatha
Was the memory of Mama!
And as a sign of his friendship,
As a token of his memory,
He decorated and adorned his pipe stem
With the crimson tuft of feathers,
With the blood-red crest of Mama.
But the wealth of Megissogwon,
All the trophies of the battle,
He shared with his people,
Shared it equally among them.

Chapter X:
Hiawatha's Wooing

"Just as the cord is to the bow,
So woman is to man;
Though she bends him, she obeys him,
Though she attracts him, she still follows him;
"Useless each without the other!"
Thus the young Hiawatha
Said to himself and thought about it,
Much confused by different emotions,
Restless, yearning, hoping, fearing,
Dreaming still of Minnehaha,
Of the beautiful Laughing Water,

In the land of the Dakotas.
"Marry a young woman from your own people,"
Warning said the old Nokomis;
"Don't go east, don't go west,"
For a stranger we don't even know!
Like a fire burning in the fireplace
Is a neighbor's plain-looking daughter,
Like the starlight or the moonlight
"Is the handsomest of strangers!"
Thus spoke Nokomis, trying to dissuade him,
And my Hiawatha answered
"Dear old Nokomis,
Very pleasant is the firelight,
But I prefer the starlight,
"I prefer the moonlight!"
Gravely then said old Nokomis:
"Don't bring an idle maiden here,"
Bring not here a useless woman,
Clumsy hands, reluctant feet;
Marry a woman with skillful hands.
Heart and hand that move together,
"Feet that eagerly run to help others!"
Hiawatha answered with a smile:
"In the land of the Dakotas"
Lives the Arrow-maker's daughter,
Minnehaha, Laughing Water,
Handsomest of all the women.
I will bring her to your wigwam,
She will take care of your errands,
Be your starlight, moonlight, firelight,
"Be the sunlight of my people!"
Still trying to discourage him, Nokomis said:
"Do not bring a stranger to my lodge"

From the land of the Dakotas!
Very fierce are the Dakotas,
Often there is conflict between us,
There are feuds that remain unforgotten,
"Wounds that ache and still may open!"
Hiawatha answered with laughter:
"For that reason, if no other,"
Would I marry the beautiful Dacotah,
That our tribes might come together as one,
That old grudges might be put aside,
"And old wounds be healed forever!"
Thus Hiawatha departed
To the land of the Dakotas,
To the land of beautiful women;
Striding across moor and meadow,
Through endless forests,
Through uninterrupted silence.
With his magical moccasins,
At every step, he covered a mile;
Yet the path ahead appeared long and daunting to him,
And his heart raced ahead of his steps;
And he traveled without stopping,
Until he heard the waterfall's laughter,
Heard the Falls of Minnehaha
Calling to him through the silence.
"What a pleasant sound!" he whispered.
"Pleasant is the voice that calls me!"
On the edges of the forests,
Between the shadow and the sunshine,
Herds of fallow deer were feeding,
But they did not see Hiawatha;
To his bow he whispered, "Don't fail me!"
"Don't miss your target!" he whispered to his arrow.

Sent it singing on its mission,
To the red heart of the deer;
Threw the deer across his shoulder,
And moved quickly ahead without stopping.
At the entrance of his tepee
The ancient Arrow-maker sat there,
In the land of the Dakotas,
Making arrowheads from jasper,
Arrow-heads made of chalcedony.
At his side, in all her beauty,
Sat the lovely Minnehaha,
Sat his daughter, Laughing Water,
Weaving mats from reeds and rushes
The old man's thoughts were focused on the past.
And the maidens of the future.
He was thinking as he sat there,
Of the days when with such arrows
He had hunted and killed the deer and bison,
On the Muskoday, the meadow;
Shot the wild goose as it flew southward
On the wing, the noisy Wawa;
Thinking of the great war-parties,
How they came to purchase his arrows,
Could not fight without his arrows.
Ah, no more such noble warriors
Could be found on earth just as they were!
Now all the men had become like women,
Only used their tongues as weapons!
She was thinking of a hunter,
From another tribe and country,
Young, tall, and strikingly handsome,
Who one morning, in the springtime,
Came to buy her father's arrows,

Sat and rested in the wigwam,
Stayed for a long time near the entrance,
Looking back as he left.
She had heard her father praise him,
Praise his courage and his wisdom;
Would he return again for arrows
To the Falls of Minnehaha?
On the mat, her hands rested motionless.
And her eyes looked very dreamy.
Through their thoughts they heard a footstep,
Heard a rustling in the branches,
And with glowing cheek and forehead,
With the deer on his shoulders,
Suddenly from out of the woodlands
Hiawatha stood before them.
Immediately the ancient Arrow-maker
Looked up seriously from his work,
Set aside the unfinished arrow,
Invited him to come in through the doorway,
As he stood up to greet him, he said,
"Hiawatha, you are welcome!"
At the feet of Laughing Water
Hiawatha set down his load,
Threw the red deer from his shoulders;
And the young woman looked up at him,
Looked up from her mat made of rushes,
Said with a gentle expression and tone,
"You are welcome, Hiawatha!"
Very spacious was the wigwam,
Made from deerskins that had been treated and bleached white,
With the Gods of the Dakotas
Drawn and painted on its curtains,
And so tall was the doorway, it was hardly

Hiawatha bent down to go inside,
Barely brushed against his eagle feathers
As he walked through the doorway.
Then the Laughing Water rose up,
From the earth, beautiful Minnehaha,
She set down her unfinished mat.
Brought forth food and set it before them,
Water brought them from the small stream,
Gave them food in clay pots,
Gave them drink in bowls made of basswood,
Listened while the guest was speaking,
Listened while her father answered,
But she never once opened her lips,
Not a single word did she speak.
Yes, she listened as if in a dream
To the words of Hiawatha,
As he spoke about old Nokomis,
Who had cared for him during his childhood,
As he spoke about his companions,
Chibiabos, the musician,
And Kwasind, the incredibly strong man,
And of happiness and abundance
In the land of the Ojibways,
In the pleasant land and peaceful.
"After many years of warfare,"
Many years of conflict and violence,
There is peace between the Ojibways
"And the tribe of the Dakotas."
Thus Hiawatha continued,
And then he added, speaking slowly,
"May this peace endure for all time,"
And let our hands be clasped more closely,
And may our hearts become more united,

Give me this young woman as my wife,
Minnehaha, Laughing Water,
"Most beautiful of Dakota women!"
And the ancient Arrow-maker
He paused for a moment before he answered,
Smoked quietly for a little while,
Gazed at Hiawatha with pride,
Fondly looked at Laughing Water,
And responded very seriously:
"Yes, if Minnehaha wishes;
"Let your heart speak, Minnehaha!"
And the beautiful Laughing Water
Seemed more lovely as she stood there,
Neither willing nor reluctant,
As she approached Hiawatha,
Gently sat down next to him,
While she spoke these words,
her cheeks reddened with embarrassment as she said them,
"I will follow you, my husband!"
This was Hiawatha's wooing!
Thus, this is how he won the daughter.
Of the ancient Arrow-maker,
In the land of the Dakotas!
From the wigwam he left,
Leading with him Laughing Water;
Hand in hand they walked together,
Through the woodland and the meadow,
Left the old man standing alone
At the entrance of his tepee,
Heard the Falls of Minnehaha
Calling out to them from far away,
Calling out to them from a great distance,
"Farewell, O Minnehaha!"

And the ancient Arrow-maker
Returned once more to his work,
Sat down by his sunny doorway,
Murmuring to himself, and saying:
"This is how our daughters leave us,"
Those we love, and those who love us!
Just when they have learned to help us,
When we grow old and depend on them,
A young man arrives wearing showy feathers,
With his reed flute, a stranger
Wanders piping through the village,
Calls to the most beautiful young woman,
And she follows wherever he guides her,
"Abandoning everything for the outsider!"
Pleasant was the journey homeward,
Through endless forests,
Over meadow, over mountain,
Over river, hill, and hollow.
Short it seemed to Hiawatha,
Though they traveled very slowly,
Though he slowed down and reduced his pace
To the steps of Laughing Water.
Over vast and rushing rivers
In his arms he carried the young woman;
Light as a feather, he thought she was,
As the feather on his hat;
Cleared the tangled pathway for her,
Pushed aside the swaying branches,
Made a shelter from branches during the night,
And a bed made of hemlock branches,
And a fire before the doorway
With the dry cones of the pine tree.
All the traveling winds accompanied them,

Over the meadows, through the forest;
All the stars of night looked at them,
Watched over their sleep with eyes that never closed;
From his hiding place in the oak tree
The squirrel, Adjidaumo, peeped,
Watched with eager eyes the lovers;
And the rabbit, the Wabasso,
Darted away from the trail ahead of them,
Looking out cautiously from his hiding place,
Sitting upright on his hind legs,
Watched the lovers with curious eyes.
Pleasant was the journey homeward!
All the birds sang loudly and sweetly.
Songs of happiness and peace of mind;
Sang the bluebird, the Owaissa,
"Happy are you, Hiawatha,"
"Having such a wife to love you!"
Sang the robin, the Opechee,
"Happy are you, Laughing Water,"
"Having such a noble husband!"
From the sky the sun shines kindly
Gazed at them through the branches,
"O my children," he said to them,
Love is sunshine, hate is shadow,
Life is a mix of dark moments and bright ones.
"Rule with love, O Hiawatha!"
From the sky, the moon gazed down at them.
Filled the lodge with mystical splendors,
Whispered to them, "O my children,
Day is restless, night is quiet,
Man domineering, woman weak;
Half belongs to me, even though I follow;
"Rule through patience, Laughing Water!"

Thus, they traveled back home;
Thus it was that Hiawatha
To the lodge of old Nokomis
Brought the moonlight, starlight, firelight,
Brought the sunshine of his people,
Minnehaha, Laughing Water,
Handsomest of all the women
In the land of the Dakotas,
In the land of beautiful women.

Chapter XI:
Hiawatha's Wedding-Feast

You will hear how Pau-Puk-Keewis,
How the Handsome Yenadizze
Danced at Hiawatha's wedding;
How the gentle Chibiabos,
He was the sweetest of all musicians,
Sang his songs of love and longing;
How Iagoo, the great boaster,
He was a marvelous storyteller,
Shared his stories of unusual adventures,
That the celebration might be more joyful,
That the time might pass more cheerfully,
And the guests will be more satisfied.
Lavish was the feast Nokomis prepared
Made at Hiawatha's wedding;
All the bowls were crafted from basswood.
White and polished very smoothly,
All the spoons made from bison horn,
Black and polished to a very smooth finish.

She had sent word throughout the entire village
Messengers carrying willow wands,
As a sign of invitation,
As a symbol of the celebration;
And the wedding guests gathered together,
Dressed in all their finest clothing,
Robes of fur and belts of wampum,
Magnificent in their colorful paint and feathers,
Beautiful with beads and tassels.
First they ate the sturgeon, Nahma,
And the pike, the Maskenozha,
Caught and cooked by old Nokomis;
Then they feasted on pemmican,
Pemmican and buffalo marrow,
Haunch of deer and hump of bison,
Yellow cakes made from Mondamin,
And the wild rice of the river.
But the kind Hiawatha,
And the beautiful Laughing Water,
And the thoughtful old Nokomis,
Didn't taste the food that was placed before them,
Only waited for the others
Only served their guests in silence.
And when all the guests had finished,
Old Nokomis, energetic and active,
From a large otter-skin pouch,
Filled the red-stone pipes for smoking
With tobacco from the South-land,
Mixed with bark from the red willow,
And with fragrant herbs and leaves.
Then she said, "O Pau-Puk-Keewis,
Dance for us your joyful dances,
Dance the Beggar's Dance to please us,

That the celebration may be more joyful,
That time may pass more cheerfully,
"And our guests be more contented!"
Then the handsome Pau-Puk-Keewis,
He the lazy Yenadizze,
He, the cheerful troublemaker,
Whom the people called the Storm-Fool,
Rose stood up among the gathered guests.
He was skilled in sports and recreational activities.
In the joyful dance of snowshoes,
In games of quoits and ball-playing;
He was skilled at gambling games.
In every game that involves skill and chance,
Pugasaing, the Bowl and Counters,
Kuntassoo, the Game of Plum-stones.
Though the warriors called him Faint-Heart,
Called him a coward, Shaugodaya,
Idler, gambler, Yenadizze,
Little did he care about their mocking.
Little did he care about their insults,
For the women and the young women
Loved the handsome Pau-Puk-Keewis.
He wore a shirt made of deerskin.
White and soft, with edges trimmed in ermine,
All intricately woven with beads of wampum;
He wore leggings made of deer skin.
Trimmed with hedgehog quills and ermine,
And in moccasins made of buckskin,
Densely decorated with quills
and beads sewn into intricate patterns.
On his head were feathers of swan's down,
On his heels were the tails of foxes,
In one hand a fan of feathers,

And he held a pipe in his other hand.
Striped with bands of red and yellow,
Streaks of blue and bright vermilion,
The face of Pau-Puk-Keewis shone brightly.
From his forehead, his hair fell down.
Smooth, and parted like a woman's,
Gleaming brilliantly with oil, and braided,
Decorated with woven strands of fragrant grasses,
As among the guests who had gathered,
To the sound of flutes and singing,
To the sound of drums and voices,
Rose the handsome Pau-Puk-Keewis,
And began his mystical dances.
First, he performed a dignified dance.
Very slow in movement and gesture,
In and out among the pine trees,
Through the shadows and the sunshine,
Treading softly like a panther.
Then faster and even faster,
Spinning, whirling around in endless circles,
Jumping over the gathered guests,
Swirling around and around the wigwam,
Until the leaves went spinning around with him,
Until the dust and wind come together
Swirled in whirlpools all around him.
Then along the sandy shore
Of the lake, the Big-Sea-Water,
He rushed forward with wild, frantic movements.
Pressed into the sand, and threw it
Wildly in the air around him;
Until the wind transformed into a whirlwind,
Until the sand was blown and sifted
Like massive snowdrifts across the landscape,

Piling sand dunes along all the coastlines,
Sand Hills of the Nagow Wudjoo!
Thus the cheerful Pau-Puk-Keewis
Performed his Beggar's Dance to entertain them,
And when he came back, he sat down laughing.
There among the gathered guests,
He sat down and calmly fanned himself.
With his fan made of turkey feathers.
Then they said to Chibiabos,
To the friend of Hiawatha,
To the sweetest of all singers,
To the greatest of all musicians,
"Sing to us, O Chibiabos!"
Songs of love and songs of longing,
That the celebration may be more joyful,
That time may pass more cheerfully,
"And our guests be more contented!"
And the gentle Chibiabos
Sang with a voice that was sweet and gentle,
Sang with deep emotional tones,
Songs of love and songs of longing;
Looking still at Hiawatha,
Looking at beautiful Laughing Water,
He sang softly, he sang in this way:
"Come away! Wake up, my beloved!"
You are the wild flower of the forest!
You, the wild bird of the prairie!
You with eyes so soft and gentle like a deer's!
"If you only look at me,
I am happy, I am happy,
As the lilies of the prairie,
When they feel the dew upon them!
"Your breath is as sweet as fragrance"

Of the wildflowers in the morning,
As their fragrance is at evening,
In the Moon when leaves are falling.
"Doesn't all the blood within me
Leap to meet you, leap to meet you,
As the springs rise to meet the sunshine,
In the Moon when nights are brightest?
"Onaway! my heart sings to thee,"
Sings with joy when you are near me,
As the sighing, singing branches
In the delightful month when strawberries ripen!
"When you are not pleased, beloved,
Then my heart becomes sad and filled with darkness,
As the gleaming river grows dark
When the clouds cast shadows on it!
"When you smile, my beloved,
Then my troubled heart becomes brighter,
As the ripples shimmer in the sunlight
That the cold wind creates in rivers.
"The earth smiles, and the waters smile,"
Cloudless skies smile down on us from above,
But I lose the ability to smile
When you are no longer near me!
"I myself, myself! behold me!"
Blood of my beating heart, behold me!
Oh wake up, wake up, my beloved!
"Come away! Wake up, my beloved!"
Thus the gentle Chibiabos
Sang his song of love and longing;
And Iagoo, the great boaster,
He was a marvelous storyteller,
He was the friend of old Nokomis,
Jealous of the sweet musician,

Envious of the praise they showered upon him,
Saw in all the eyes around him,
Saw in all their looks and gestures,
That the wedding guests gathered together
Yearned to listen to his delightful tales,
His countless lies.
Very boastful was Iagoo;
He had never heard of such an adventure.
But he himself had encountered someone greater;
Never any deed of daring
But he himself had done something even bolder;
Never any amazing story
But he could tell a stranger himself.
Would you listen to his bragging,
Would you just believe him,
No one has ever shot an arrow
Half as far and high as he had;
Ever caught so many fish,
Ever killed so many reindeer,
Ever trapped so many beaver!
No one could run as fast as he could.
No one could dive as deep as he could.
No one could swim as far as he could;
None had traveled so many times,
None had witnessed so many marvels,
As this wonderful Iagoo,
As this marvelous storyteller!
Thus his name became a common expression
And a joke among the people;
And whenever a boastful hunter
Praised his own skill too much,
Or a warrior returning home,
Spoke excessively about his accomplishments,

All his listeners shouted, "Iagoo!"
"Here comes Iagoo among us!"
He was the one who carved the cradle
Of the little Hiawatha,
Carved its framework out of linden,
Bound it tightly with reindeer sinews;
He was the one who taught him later
How to make his bows and arrows,
How to Make Bows from Ash Wood
And the arrows of the oak tree.
So among the guests who had gathered
At my Hiawatha's wedding
Sat Iagoo, old and ugly,
Sat the marvelous storyteller.
And they said, "O good Iagoo,
Tell us now a story of wonder,
Tell us about some unusual adventure.
That the celebration may be more joyful,
That time may pass more cheerfully,
"And our guests be more contented!"
And Iagoo responded immediately,
"You will hear a remarkable story,"
You will hear about the strange adventures
Of Osseo, the Magician,
"From the Evening Star descending."

———————

Chapter XII:
The Son of the Evening Star

Can it be the sun setting
Over the level plain of water?
Or the Red Swan floating, flying,
Wounded by the magic arrow,
Turning all the waves a deep red color,
With the crimson of its life-blood,
Filling all the air with splendor,
With the magnificence of its feathers?
Yes; it is the sun setting.
Sinking down into the water;
All the sky is stained with purple,
All the water turned bright red!
No; it is the Red Swan floating,
Diving down beneath the water;
To the sky its wings are lifted,
With its blood the waves are reddened!
Over it the Star of Evening
Melts and trembles through the purple,
Hangs suspended in the twilight.
No; it is a bead of wampum
On the robes of the Great Spirit
As he moves through the twilight,
Walks in silence through the heavens.
This sight filled Iagoo with joy as he watched
And he said quickly: "Look at it!"
See the sacred Star of Evening!
You will hear an amazing story.
Hear the story of Osseo,
Son of the Evening Star, Osseo!

"Once, in days no longer remembered,"
Ages closer to the beginning,
When the heavens were closer to us,
And the Gods were more familiar,
In the northern lands lived a hunter,
With ten young and beautiful daughters,
Tall and slender like willow branches;
Only Oweenee, the youngest,
She, the stubborn and unpredictable one,
She, the quiet, thoughtful young woman,
Was the most beautiful of the sisters.
"All these women married warriors,"
Married courageous and proud husbands;
Only Oweenee, the youngest,
Laughed at and mocked all her lovers,
All her young and handsome suitors,
And then she married old Osseo,
Old Osseo, poor and ugly,
Worn down by age and weakened by coughing,
Always coughing like a squirrel.
"Ah, but beautiful within him"
Was the spirit of Osseo,
From the Evening Star descended,
Star of Evening, Star of Woman,
Star of tenderness and passion!
All its fire burned within his chest,
All its beauty in his spirit,
All its mystery exists within his very being,
All its splendor in his language!
"And her lovers, the rejected,
Handsome men wearing belts made of wampum,
Attractive men adorned with paint and feathers.
Pointed at her mockingly,

Followed her with jokes and laughter.
But she said: 'I don't care about you,
Care nothing for your belts of wampum,
Care nothing for your makeup and decorative ornaments,
Care nothing for your jokes and laughter;
"I am happy with Osseo!"
"Once invited to some grand celebration,"
Through the humid twilight of evening,
Walked together the ten sisters,
Walked alongside their husbands;
Slowly followed old Osseo,
With beautiful Oweenee beside him;
All the others chatted cheerfully,
These two walked in silence.
"At the western sky Osseo
Stared intently, as if pleading,
Often stopped and gazed with pleading eyes
At the shimmering Evening Star,
At the gentle beginning of womanhood;
And they heard him whisper quietly,
[missing text]
"Pity, pity me, my father!"
"'Listen!' said the eldest sister,
"He is praying to his father!"
What a shame that the elderly man
Does not trip along the way,
"Doesn't break his neck by falling!"
And they laughed until the entire forest
echoed with their laughter.
Echoed with their inappropriate laughter.
"On their pathway through the woodlands"
Place an oak tree that storms have torn from the ground,
Place the massive trunk of an oak tree,

Buried halfway beneath leaves and moss,
Decaying, crumbling, massive and empty.
And when Osseo saw it,
Gave a shout, a cry of anguish,
Jumped into its gaping cave,
At one end, an old man entered.
Wasted, wrinkled, old, and ugly;
From the other direction came a young man,
Tall and straight and strong and handsome.
"In this way, Osseo was transformed,"
Thus restored to youth and beauty;
But sadly for good Osseo,
And for Oweenee, the faithful!
Strangely, she was also transformed.
Changed into a frail elderly woman,
With a walking stick, she hobbled forward,
Wasted, wrinkled, old, and ugly!
And the sisters and their husbands
Laughed until the echoing forest
Echoed with their inappropriate laughter.
"But Osseo did not turn away from her,"
Walked with slower steps beside her,
Took her hand, which was brown and weathered
As an oak leaf is in winter,
Called her sweetheart, Nenemoosha,
Comforted her with gentle, caring words,
Until they arrived at the feast hall,
Until they sat down in the wigwam,
Sacred to the Star of Evening,
To the gentle Star of Woman.
"Lost in visions, absorbed in dreaming,"
At the banquet sat Osseo;
All were cheerful, all were joyful,

All were joyful except Osseo.
Neither food nor drink did he taste,
Neither did he speak nor listen;
But there he sat, completely bewildered,
Looking with a dreamy and sad expression,
First at Oweenee, then upward
At the bright sky above them.
"Then a voice was heard, a whisper,
Coming from the starry distance,
Coming from the empty vastness,
Low, musical, and tender;
And the voice said: "O Osseo!"
O my son, my most beloved!
Broken are the spells that bound you,
All the charms of the magicians,
All the magical forces of evil;
"Come to me; ascend, Osseo!"
"'Taste the food that stands before you:
It is blessed and enchanted,
It possesses magical powers within it.
It will transform you into a spirit.
All your bowls and all your kettles
Shall be wood and clay no longer;
But the bowls were changed to wampum,
And the kettles shall be silver;
They will gleam like bright red shells,
Like fire that shines and flickers.
"'And the women shall no longer
Bear the grim burden of work,
But be transformed into birds, and shine
With the beauty of the starlight,
Painted with the dusky splendors
Of the skies and clouds of evening!'

"What Osseo heard as whispers,
What he understood through words,
Was nothing more than music to the others,
Music like distant birdsong,
Of the whippoorwill in the distance,
Of the Lonely Wawonaissa
Singing in the dark forest.
"Then the lodge began to tremble,
Immediately began to shake and tremble,
And they felt it rising, rising,
Slowly rising through the air,
From the darkness of the treetops
Forth into the dewy starlight,
Until it passed the highest branches;
And look! the wooden dishes
All were transformed into scarlet shells!
And look! the clay pots
All were changed to bowls of silver!
And the roof-poles of the wigwam
Were like gleaming silver rods,
And the bark roof above them
As the gleaming fragments of beetles.
"Then Osseo looked around him,
And he saw the nine beautiful sisters,
All the sisters and their husbands,
Changed into birds with different colored feathers.
Some were jays and some were magpies,
Others are thrushes, others are blackbirds;
And they hopped, and sang, and chirped,
Raised and ruffled all their feathers,
Showed off in their gleaming feathers,
And their tails spread out like fans.
"Only Oweenee, the youngest,

Was not changed, but sat in silence,
Wasted, wrinkled, old, and ugly,
Looking sadly at the others;
Until Osseo, looking upward,
Gave another cry of anguish,
Such a cry as he had let out
By the oak tree in the forest.
"Then her youth and beauty returned,"
And her dirty and torn clothes
Were transformed into robes of ermine,
And her staff transformed into a feather,
Yes, a shining silver feather!
"And once again the wigwam shook,"
Carried and swept through flowing air currents,
Through clear clouds and mist,
And amid celestial splendors
On the Evening Star alighted,
As one snowflake falls upon another,
As a leaf falls onto a river,
As the thistledown on water.
"Come forward with cheerful words of welcome"
The father of Osseo came,
He with shining silver hair,
He with calm and gentle eyes.
And he said: 'My son, Osseo,
Hang the birdcage you bring there,
Hang the cage with rods of silver,
And the birds with shimmering feathers,
At the entrance of my wigwam.
"At the door he hung the bird-cage,"
And they went in and joyfully
Listened to Osseo's father,
Ruler of the Star of Evening,

As he said: 'O my Osseo!'
I have felt compassion for you,
Given back your youth and beauty,
Into birds with different colored feathers
Changed your sisters and their husbands;
Changed them this way because they ridiculed you
In the figure of the old man,
In that sorrowful and lined face,
Could not see your passionate heart,
Could not see your youth as immortal;
Only Oweenee, the faithful,
Saw your naked heart and loved you.
"'In the lodge that shines over there,
In the little star that twinkles
Through the mist, on the left side,
Lives the envious Evil Spirit,
The Wabeno, the magician,
Who changed you into an old man.
Be careful not to let his rays shine upon you,
For the light he radiates around him
Are the power of his enchantment,
"Are the arrows that he uses."
"Many years, in peace and quiet,"
On the Peaceful Evening Star
Osseo lived with his father;
Many years passed in song and celebration.
At the entrance of the wigwam,
Hung the cage with rods of silver,
And beautiful Oweenee, the faithful,
Gave birth to a son for Osseo,
With the beauty of his mother,
With the courage of his father.
"And the boy grew up and prospered,"

And Osseo, to bring him joy,
Made him small bows and arrows,
Opened the great cage of silver,
And set free his aunts and uncles,
All those birds with shiny feathers,
For his little son to shoot at.
"Round and round they spun and swooped,"
Filled the Evening Star with music,
With their songs of joy and freedom
Filled the Evening Star with splendor,
With the rustling of their feathers;
Until the boy, the young hunter,
Bent his bow and shot an arrow,
Shot a quick and deadly arrow,
And a bird, with gleaming feathers,
At his feet, the wounded fell in great pain.
"But what an amazing transformation!
It was no bird he saw before him,
It was a beautiful young woman,
With the arrow piercing her chest!
"When her blood fell on the planet,
On the sacred Evening Star,
Broken was the spell of magic,
Powerless was the strange enchantment,
And the young man, the fearless archer,
Suddenly he felt himself falling.
Gripped by invisible forces, yet falling
Downward through the empty spaces,
Downward through the clouds and vapors,
Until he came to rest on an island,
On an island, green and grassy,
Yonder in the Big-Sea-Water.
"After him he saw descending

All the birds with gleaming feathers,
Fluttering, falling, drifting downward,
Like the painted leaves of autumn;
And the lodge with poles of silver,
With its roof resembling the wings of beetles,
Like the gleaming fragments of beetles,
By the winds of heaven uplifted,
Slowly sank upon the island,
Bringing back the good Osseo,
Bringing Oweenee, the faithful.
"Then the birds, transformed once more,"
Took on human form once again,
Took their form, but not their size;
They stayed as Little People,
Like the pygmies, the Puk-Wudjies,
And on pleasant summer nights,
When the Evening Star was shining,
Hand in hand they danced together
On the island's rugged cliffs,
On the low, level sandy beach.
"You can still see their shining lodge there,"
On peaceful summer evenings,
And on the shore the fisherman
Sometimes hears their happy voices,
"Sees them dancing in the starlight!"
When the story was finished,
When the amazing story came to an end,
Looking around at his audience,
Solemnly Iagoo added:
"There are great men, I have known such,"
Whom their people do not understand,
Whom they even make a joke of,
Mock and ridicule with contempt.

From the story of Osseo
"Let us learn the fate of jesters!"
All the wedding guests were delighted
Listened to the wonderful story,
Listened while laughing and applauding,
And they whispered to each other:
"Does he mean himself, I wonder?"
"And are we the aunts and uncles?"
Then Chibiabos sang once more,
Sang a song of love and longing,
In those sweet and gentle tones,
In those tones of thoughtful melancholy,
A young woman sang her sorrowful song
For her lover, her Algonquin.
"When I think of my beloved,
Ah me! think of my beloved,
When my heart is thinking of him,
O my sweetheart, my Algonquin!
"Oh, how I felt when I had to leave him!"
Around my neck he placed the wampum,
As a pledge, the snow-white wampum,
O my sweetheart, my Algonquin!
"'I'll come with you,' he whispered,"
"Oh, how I long for your homeland!"
"Let me come with you," he whispered.
"Oh my darling, my Algonquin!"
"Far away, away," I replied,
"Very far away," I replied.
"Oh, this is my homeland!"
"Oh my darling, my Algonquin!"
"When I turned around to look at him,
Where we said goodbye, to see him,
After me he continued to stare,

O my sweetheart, my Algonquin!
"He was still standing by the tree,"
By the fallen tree was standing,
That had fallen into the water,
O my sweetheart, my Algonquin!
"When I think of my beloved,
Ah me! think of my beloved,
When my heart is thinking of him,
"Oh my darling, my Algonquin!"
Such was Hiawatha's Wedding,
Such was the dance of Pau-Puk-Keewis,
Such is the story of Iagoo,
Such were the songs of Chibiabos;
Thus the wedding banquet came to an end,
And the wedding guests left.
Leaving Hiawatha happy
With the night and Minnehaha.

Chapter XIII:
Blessing the Cornfields

Sing, O Song of Hiawatha,
Of the happy days that came after,
In the land of the Ojibways,
In the pleasant land and peaceful!
Sing the mysteries of Mondamin,
Sing the Blessing of the Cornfields!
The bloody hatchet was buried.
Buried was the terrible war club,
All weapons of war were buried.
And the war-cry was forgotten.

There was peace among the nations;
The hunters roamed undisturbed,
Built the birch canoe for sailing,
Caught the fish in lake and river,
Shot the deer and trapped the beaver;
The women worked without being disturbed.
Made their sugar from the maple,
Collected wild rice from the meadows,
Dressed in the skins of deer and beaver.
All around the joyful village
The cornfields stood there, green and gleaming,
Waved the green plumes of Mondamin,
Waved his soft and golden hair,
Filling all the land with abundance.
It was the women who in springtime
Planted the vast fields and fertile,
Mondamin was buried in the earth;
It was the women who in autumn
Removed the golden outer shells from the harvest,
Stripped the clothes from Mondamin,
Even as Hiawatha taught them.
Once, when all the corn was planted,
Hiawatha, wise and thoughtful,
Spoke and said to Minnehaha,
To his wife, the Laughing Water:
"You will bless the cornfields tonight,"
Draw a magic circle around them,
To protect them from destruction,
Blast of mildew, blight of insect,
Wagemin, the thief of cornfields,
Paimosaid, who steals the corn cob.
"At night, when everything is silent,"
In the night, when everything is dark,

When the Spirit of Sleep, Nepahwin,
Closes the doors of all the wigwams,
So that not a single ear can hear you,
So that no one can see you,
Rise up from your bed in silence,
Set aside all of your clothing completely.
Walk through the fields you planted,
Around the edges of the grain fields,
Covered only by your flowing hair,
Clothed in darkness like a robe.
"This way the fields will be more productive,"
And the sound of your footsteps fading away
Draw a magic circle around them,
So that neither disease nor decay,
Neither burrowing worm nor insect,
Shall pass over the magic circle;
Not the dragonfly, Kwo-ne-she,
Nor the spider, Subbekashe,
Nor the grasshopper, Pah-puk-keena;
Nor the mighty caterpillar,
Way-muk-kwana, with the bear-skin,
"King of all the caterpillars!"
On the treetops near the cornfields
The hungry crows and ravens perched there,
Kahgahgee, the King of Ravens,
With his gang of black raiders.
And they laughed at Hiawatha,
Until the treetops trembled with laughter,
With their sad laughter,
At the words of Hiawatha.
"Listen to him!" they said; "listen to the Wise Man!"
"Listen to the stories of Hiawatha!"
When the silent night fell

Broad and dark over field and forest,
When the sorrowful Wawonaissa
Grief sang among the hemlock trees,
And the Spirit of Sleep, Nepahwin,
Close the doors of all the wigwams,
From her bed, Laughing Water rose.
She completely removed her clothing.
And cloaked and protected by darkness,
Unashamed and unafraid,
Walked safely around the cornfields,
Drew the sacred, magic circle
Of her footprints around the cornfields.
No one except Midnight alone
Saw her beauty in the darkness,
No one except the Wawonaissa
Heard the rapid breathing from her chest
Guskewau, the darkness, enveloped her
Wrapped tightly in his sacred mantle,
So that no one could see her beauty,
So that no one could brag, "I saw her!"
The next morning, as daylight broke,
Kahgahgee, the King of Ravens,
Assembled all his dark raiders,
Crows and blackbirds, jays and ravens,
Noisy in the darkening treetops,
And descended, fast and fearless,
On the fields of Hiawatha,
On the grave of the Mondamin.
"We will drag Mondamin," they said,
"From the grave where he is buried,"
Despite all the magic circles
Laughing Water draws around it,
Despite all the sacred footprints

"Minnehaha stamps upon it!"
But the cautious Hiawatha,
Ever thoughtful, careful, and watchful,
Had overheard the scornful laughter
When they ridiculed him from the treetops.
"Caw!" he said, "my friends the ravens!"
Kahgahgee, my King of Ravens!
I will teach you all a lesson
"That won't be forgotten anytime soon!"
He had gotten up before dawn.
He had spread across all the cornfields
Traps to capture the black raiders,
And was now lying in wait
In the nearby grove of pine trees,
Waiting for the crows and blackbirds,
Waiting for the jays and ravens.
Soon they arrived with loud cawing and commotion,
Rush of wings and cry of voices,
To their work of destruction,
Settling down upon the cornfields,
Digging deep with beak and claw,
For the body of Mondamin.
And despite all their skill and cleverness,
All their expertise in the cunning tactics of war,
They didn't see any danger close to them.
Until their claws became tangled together,
Until they discovered they were trapped
In the traps of Hiawatha.
From his hiding place he emerged,
Striding terrible among them,
And his appearance was so terrifying
That even the bravest were overcome with terror.
Without mercy he destroyed them

Right and left, in groups of ten and twenty,
And their miserable, dead bodies
Suspended high on poles as scarecrows
Around the sacred grain fields,
As a sign of his revenge,
As a warning to raiders.
Only Kahgahgee, the leader,
Kahgahgee, the King of Ravens,
He was the only one among them who survived.
As a hostage for his people.
With his rope for binding prisoners, he tied him up.
Led him captive to his wigwam,
Bound him tightly with ropes made from elm bark
To the ridge-pole of his wigwam.
"Kahgahgee, my raven!" he said,
"You the leader of the robbers,
You who planned this trouble,
The person who planned this outrage,
I will keep you, I will hold you,
As a hostage for your people,
"As a promise of good conduct!"
And he left him, grim and sulky,
Sitting in the morning sunshine
On the top of the wigwam,
Croaking loudly to show his anger,
Beating his enormous black wings,
Struggling in vain for his freedom,
Calling out to his people in vain!
Summer passed, and Shawondasee
Breathed his sighs across the entire landscape,
From the southern lands came his passionate fire,
Gentle kisses carried on the breeze, warm and tender;
And the cornfield grew and ripened,

Until it stood in all its splendor
Of its green and yellow garments,
Of its tassels and its plumage,
And the corn ears full and gleaming
Gleamed from bursting sheaths of green foliage.
Then Nokomis, the old woman,
Spoke, and said to Minnehaha:
"'Tis the Moon when leaves are falling;"
All the wild rice has been gathered,
And the corn is ripe and ready;
Let us gather in the harvest,
Let us wrestle with Mondamin,
Remove his decorative feathers and ornamental fringes.
"Of his garments green and yellow!"
And the cheerful Laughing Water
Went rejoicing from the wigwam,
With Nokomis, old and wrinkled,
And they gathered the women around them,
Called the young men and the maidens,
To the harvest of the cornfields,
To the husking of the corn.
On the edge of the forest,
Beneath the sweet-scented pine trees,
The old men and warriors sat there.
Smoking in the pleasant shade.
In uninterrupted silence
They looked at the playful work
Of the young men and the women;
Listened to their loud chatter,
To their laughter and their singing,
Heard them chattering like the magpies,
Heard them laughing like the blue jays,
Heard them singing like the robins.

And whenever some fortunate young woman
Found a red ear while husking corn.
Found a corn cob red as blood,
"Nushka!" they all cried out together,
"Nushka! you shall have a sweetheart,"
"You're going to have a handsome husband!"
"Ugh!" all the old men replied
From their seats beneath the pine trees.
And whenever a young man or woman
Found a bent ear while husking corn.
Found a corn cob while husking
Damaged, diseased, or deformed,
Then they laughed and sang together,
Crawled and hobbled through the grain fields,
Copied in their walk and movements
Some elderly man, hunched over and nearly folded in half,
Singing alone or with others:
"Wagemin, the thief of cornfields!"
"Paimo said, who steals the corn!"
Until the cornfields echoed with laughter,
Until from Hiawatha's wigwam
Kahgahgee, the King of Ravens,
Screamed and trembled with rage,
And from all the nearby treetops
The black raiders cawed and croaked.
"Ugh!" all the old men replied,
From their seats beneath the pine trees!

———————

Chapter XIV:
Picture-Writing

In those days, Hiawatha said,
"Look! How everything fades away and dies!"
From the memories of the elderly
Pass away the great traditions,
The accomplishments of the fighters,
The adventures of the hunters,
All the wisdom of the Medes,
All the skill of the Wabenos,
All the wonderful dreams and visions
Of the Jossakeeds, the Prophets!
"Great men die and are forgotten,"
Wise people speak; their words carry wisdom
Perish in the ears that hear them,
Do not reach the generations
That, as yet unborn, are waiting
In the vast, enigmatic darkness
Of the silent days that are yet to come!
"On the grave-posts of our fathers"
Are there no signs or painted figures?
Who lies buried in those graves remains unknown to us.
Only know they are our fathers.
Of what family they belong to and what their lineage is,
From what ancient, ancestral Totem,
Be it Eagle, Bear, or Beaver,
They went down, though we don't know this for certain.
Only know they are our fathers.
"Face to face we speak together,"
But we cannot speak when we are not present,
Cannot send our voices from us

To the friends who live far away;
Cannot send a secret message,
But the messenger discovers our secret,
May corrupt it, may betray it,
"May reveal it unto others."
Thus spoke Hiawatha, walking
In the lonely forest,
Thinking deeply, reflecting in the woods,
On the welfare of his people.
From his pouch he took his colors,
Took his paints of different colors,
On the smooth bark of a birch tree
Painted many shapes and figures,
Wonderful and mystic figures,
And each figure had a meaning,
Each word or thought sparked a suggestion.
Gitche Manito the Mighty,
He, the Master of Life, was painted
As an egg, with points sticking out
To the four winds of the heavens.
Everywhere is the Great Spirit,
Was the meaning of this symbol.
Mitche Manito the Mighty,
He is the terrifying Spirit of Evil,
As a serpent was depicted,
As Kenabeek, the great serpent.
Very clever, very cunning,
Is the creeping Spirit of Evil,
Was the meaning of this symbol.
Life and Death he depicted as circles,
Life was bright and pure, but Death was shrouded in darkness;
Sun and moon and stars he painted,
Man and beast, fish and reptile,

Forests, mountains, lakes, and rivers.
For the earth he drew a straight line,
For the sky, a bow arches above it;
White the space between for daytime,
Filled with little stars for nighttime;
On the left, there's a point marking where the sun rises.
On the right, there's a spot for watching the sunset.
At the top, a point marking noon,
And for rainy and cloudy weather
Wavy lines flowing downward from it.
Footprints pointing towards a wigwam
Were a sign of invitation,
Were a sign of guests gathering;
Bloody hands with palms uplifted
Were a symbol of destruction,
Were a hostile sign and symbol.
All these things Hiawatha accomplished
Show his amazed people,
And explained what they meant,
And he said: "Look, your grave markers"
Have no mark, no sign, nor symbol,
Go and paint them all with figures;
Each one with its household symbol,
With its own ancestral Totem;
So that those who come after
"May distinguish them and know them."
And they painted on the grave-posts
On the graves not yet forgotten,
Each person has their own ancestral Totem,
Each one representing the symbol of their household;
Figures of the Bear and Reindeer,
Of the Turtle, Crane, and Beaver,
Each one turned upside down as a symbol

The owner had left.
That the leader who carried the emblem
Lay beneath in dust and ashes.
And the Jossakeeds, the Prophets,
The Wabenos, the Magicians,
And the Medicine-men, the Medas,
Painted on bark and deerskin
Figures for the songs they sang,
For each song a separate symbol,
Mysterious and awe-inspiring figures,
Figures strange and brightly colored;
And each figure had its meaning,
Each one suggested some magical song.
The Great Spirit, the Creator,
Brilliant light blazing across the entire sky;
The Great Serpent, the Kenabeek,
With his blood-red crest raised high,
Crawling, gazing up into heaven;
In the sky the sun, that listens,
And the moon eclipsed and dying;
Owl and eagle, crane and hen-hawk,
And the cormorant, bird of magic;
Headless men who walk through the heavens,
Bodies lying pierced with arrows,
Bloodstained hands of death raised high,
Flags on graves, and great war-captains
Grasping both the earth and heaven!
Such were the forms they depicted
On birch bark and deerskin;
Songs of war and songs of hunting,
Songs of medicine and of magic,
All were written using these symbols.
For each figure had its meaning,

Each song was recorded separately.
Nor was the Love-Song forgotten,
The most subtle of all medicines,
The most powerful magical spell,
Dangerous more than war or hunting!
Thus the Love-Song was recorded,
Symbol and interpretation.
First a human figure standing,
Painted in the brightest scarlet;
It is the lover, the musician,
And the meaning is, "My painting
"Makes me powerful over others."
Then the figure sat down and began singing,
Playing on a drum of magic,
And the interpretation, "Listen!"
"It's my voice you hear, my singing!"
Then the same red figure sat down
In the shelter of a wigwam,
And the meaning of the symbol,
"I will come and sit beside you"
"In the mystery of my passion!"
Then two figures appeared, a man and a woman,
Standing hand in hand together
With their hands clasped tightly together
That they appeared as one unified whole,
And the words represented in this way
"I can see into your heart,"
"And your cheeks are red with blushes!"
Next, the maiden found herself on an island,
In the center of an island;
And the song this shape suggested
Though you were far away,
Were upon some far-off island,

Such is the spell I cast upon you,
Such is the magical power of passion,
"I could immediately draw you to me!"
Then the figure of the young woman
Sleeping, with her lover beside her,
Whispering to her while she sleeps,
Saying, "Though you were far from me
In the realm of Sleep and Silence,
"Still the voice of love would reach you!"
And the final figure of them all
Was a heart within a circle,
Drawn within a magic circle;
And the image had this meaning:
"Your heart lies naked before me,"
"To your naked heart I whisper!"
Thus it was that Hiawatha,
In his wisdom, he taught the people
All the mysteries of painting,
All the art of Picture-Writing,
On the smooth bark of the birch tree,
On the white skin of the reindeer,
On the grave markers of the village.

Chapter XV:
Hiawatha's Lamentation

In those days the Evil Spirits,
All the spirits of mischief,
Fearing Hiawatha's wisdom,
And his love for Chibiabos,
Envious of their loyal friendship,

And their noble words and actions,
Made at length a league against them,
To harass them and destroy them.
Hiawatha, wise and cautious,
Often said to Chibiabos,
"Oh my brother! Please don't leave me,"
"May the Evil Spirits not harm you!"
Chibiabos, young and careless,
Laughter made his jet-black hair shake.
Answered always sweet and childlike,
"Don't be afraid for me, O brother!"
"Harm and evil cannot touch me!"
Once when Peboan, the Winter,
Covered with ice, the great lake stretched out,
When the snowflakes swirl downward,
Whispered through the dried oak leaves,
Changed the pine trees into wigwams,
Covered all the earth with silence,
Armed with arrows and wearing snowshoes,
Ignoring his brother's warning,
Fearing not the Evil Spirits,
Heading out to hunt the antlered deer
All alone went Chibiabos.
Right across the vast ocean
The deer leaped swiftly ahead of him.
With the wind and snow he followed,
Over the treacherous ice he followed,
Wild with all the intense turmoil
And the ecstasy of the hunt.
But beneath, the Evil Spirits
Lay in ambush, waiting for him,
Broke the treacherous ice beneath him,
Pulled him down to the depths,

His body was buried in the sand.
Unktahee, the god of water,
He, the god of the Dakotas,
Drowned him in the deep abysses
Of Lake Gitche Gumee.
From the headlands Hiawatha
Sent out such a cry of pain,
Such a terrifying cry of grief,
That the bison stopped to listen,
And the wolves howled from the prairies,
And the thunder in the distance
Starting answered "Baim-wawa!"
Then he painted his face black,
With his robe, he covered his head.
In his wigwam he sat lamenting,
Seven long weeks he sat in sorrow,
Uttering still this moan of sorrow:
"He is dead, the sweet musician!"
He was the sweetest of all singers!
He has left us forever,
He has moved a little closer.
To the Master of all music,
To the Master of all singing!
"O my brother, Chibiabos!"
And the melancholy fir trees
Waved their dark green fans above him,
Waved their purple cones above him,
Sighing alongside him to comfort him,
Mixing with his grief
Their complaints and their sorrows.
When spring arrived, the entire forest
Searched everywhere for Chibiabos without success;
Sighed the rivulet, Sebowisha,

The rushes in the meadow sighed.
From the treetops, the bluebird sang,
Sang the bluebird, the Owaissa,
"Chibiabos! Chibiabos!"
"He is dead, the sweet musician!"
From the wigwam sang the robin,
Sang the robin, the Opechee,
"Chibiabos! Chibiabos!"
"He is dead, the sweetest singer!"
And at night through all the forest
The whippoorwill went on complaining,
The Wawonaissa wailed,
"Chibiabos! Chibiabos!"
He is dead, the sweet musician!
"He is the sweetest of all singers!"
Then the Medicine-men, the Medas,
The magicians, the Wabenos,
And the Jossakeeds, the Prophets,
Came to visit Hiawatha;
Built a Sacred Lodge beside him,
To calm him down, to comfort him,
Walked in silent, solemn procession,
Carrying each a bag of healing,
Beaver, lynx, or otter fur,
Filled with magical roots and herbs,
Filled with very powerful medicines.
When he heard their footsteps getting closer,
Hiawatha stopped grieving,
Called no more on Chibiabos;
Nothing he questioned, nothing he answered,
But with his sorrowful head bare,
From his face, the colors of mourning
He washed slowly and in silence,

Slowly and in silence they followed
Onward to the Sacred Wigwam.
There they gave him a magic drink,
Made from Nahma-wusk, the spearmint,
And Wabeno-wusk, the yarrow,
Roots of power, and herbs of healing;
Beat their drums and shook their rattles;
Sung individually and as a group,
Mystic songs like these, they chanted.
"I myself, myself! behold me!"
"It is the great Gray Eagle speaking;"
Come, you white crows, come and listen to him!
The thunderous roar assists me;
All the invisible spirits assist me;
I can hear their voices calling,
All around the sky I hear them!
I can blow you strong, my brother,
"I can heal you, Hiawatha!"
"Hi-au-ha!" the chorus responded,
"Wayha-way!" the mystic chorus chanted.
Friends of mine are all the serpents!
Hear me shake my skin of hen-hawk!
Mahng, the white loon, I can kill him;
I can shoot your heart and kill it!
I can blow you strong, my brother,
"I can heal you, Hiawatha!"
"Hi-au-ha!" the chorus responded,
"Wayhaway!" the mystic chorus.
"I myself, myself! the prophet!"
When I speak, the wigwam trembles.
Shakes the Sacred Lodge with terror,
Invisible hands start to shake it!
When I walk, I step upon the sky

Bends and makes a noise beneath me!
"I can make you strong, my brother!"
"Rise and speak, O Hiawatha!"
"Hi-au-ha!" the chorus responded,
"Way-ha-way!" the mystical chorus chanted.
Then they shook their medicine bags
Over the head of Hiawatha,
Danced their healing dance around him;
And jumping up wild and disheveled,
Like someone waking up from a dream,
He was cured of all his insanity.
As the clouds are swept from heaven,
Immediately his mind cleared
All his brooding sadness;
As the ice is cleared from rivers,
Immediately his heart was freed
All his sorrow and suffering.
Then they called for Chibiabos
From his grave beneath the waters,
From the shores of Gitche Gumee
Hiawatha's brother was called forth.
And so powerful was the magic
Of that cry and invocation,
That he heard it while lying there
Beneath the Great Waters;
From the sand he rose and listened,
Heard the music and the singing,
Came, obedient to the summons,
To the entrance of the wigwam,
But they forbade him to enter.
Through a crack they gave him a piece of coal.
Through the door came a blazing torch;
Ruler in the Land of Spirits,

Ruler over the dead, they made him,
Telling him to light a fire
For everyone who died after that,
Camp fires for their nighttime encampments
On their solitary journey
To the kingdom of Ponemah,
To the land of the Hereafter.
From the village where he grew up,
From the homes of those who knew him,
Passing silently through the forest,
Like smoke drifting to one side,
Slowly Chibiabos vanished!
Where he walked, the branches didn't move,
Where he walked, the grass didn't bend beneath his feet,
And the fallen leaves of last year
Made no sound beneath his footstep.
Four entire days he traveled forward
Down the pathway of the dead men;
On the dead man's strawberry they feasted,
Crossed the sorrowful river,
On the swinging log he crossed it,
Came to the Lake of Silver,
In the Stone Canoe was carried
To the Islands of the Blessed,
To the land of ghosts and shadows.
On that journey, moving slowly,
Many tired souls he witnessed,
Breathing heavily under heavy loads,
Carrying war clubs, bows and arrows,
Robes made of fur, along with pots and kettles,
And with food that friends had provided
For that solitary journey.
"Yes! Why do the living," they said,

"Place such heavy burdens on us!"
Better to go naked,
Better to go without food,
Then to bear such heavy burdens
"On our long and exhausting journey!"
Then Hiawatha came forth,
Wandered eastward, wandered westward,
Teaching People How to Use Simple Remedies
And the remedies for poisons,
And the cure of all diseases.
Thus, this was first revealed to humanity.
All the mystery of Medamin,
All the sacred art of healing.

Chapter XVI:
Pau-Puk-Keewis

You will hear how Pau-Puk-Keewis,
He, the handsome Yenadizze,
Whom the people called the Storm-Fool,
Troubled the village with chaos;
You will hear about all his troublemaking.
And his escape from Hiawatha,
And his amazing transformations,
And the end of his adventures.
On the shores of Gitche Gumee,
On the dunes of Nagow Wudjoo,
By the gleaming Great Water
Stood the lodge of Pau-Puk-Keewis.
It was he who in his madness
Swirled these shifting sands together,

On the dunes of Nagow Wudjoo,
When the guests had gathered together,
He was so cheerful and wildly enthusiastic
Danced at Hiawatha's wedding,
Performed the Beggar's Dance to satisfy them.
Now, looking for new adventures,
From his lodge went Pau-Puk-Keewis,
Arrived quickly in the village,
Found all the young men gathered together
In the lodge of old Iagoo,
Listening to his horrifying tales,
To his wonderful adventures.
He was telling them the story
Of Ojeeg, the Summer-Maker,
How he made a hole in heaven,
How he ascended to heaven,
And let out the summer weather,
The endless, delightful Summer;
How the Otter First Attempted It
How the Beaver, Lynx, and Badger
Attempted in succession the remarkable accomplishment,
From the top of the mountain
Struck their fists against the heavens,
Struck their foreheads against the sky,
Cracked the sky, but could not break it;
How the Wolverine rose up,
Made him ready for the encounter,
Bent his knees down, like a squirrel,
Drew his arms back, like a cricket.
"Once he leaped," said old Iagoo,
"Once he leaped, and look! above him"
The sky curved like ice forming in rivers
When the waters rise beneath it;

Twice he jumped, and look! above him
Cracked the sky, as ice in rivers
When the flood is at its peak!
Three times he jumped, and look! above him
Broke the shattered sky apart,
And he disappeared within it,
And Ojeeg, the Fisher Weasel,
"With a leap, he went in behind him!"
"Listen up!" shouted Pau-Puk-Keewis
As he walked through the doorway;
"I'm exhausted by all this conversation."
Tired of old Iagoo's stories,
Tired of Hiawatha's wisdom.
Here is something to entertain you,
"Better than this endless talking."
Then from his wolf-skin pouch
He stepped forward with a serious, dignified bearing.
All the game of Bowl and Counters,
Pugasaing, with thirteen pieces.
White on one side, they were painted.
And vermilion on the other;
Two Kenabeeks or great serpents,
Two Ininewug or wedge-men,
One great war-club, Pugamaugun,
And one slender fish, the Keego,
Four round pieces, Ozawabeeks,
And three Sheshebwug or ducklings.
All were made of bone and painted.
All except the Ozawabeeks;
These were made of brass, polished bright on one side.
And were black on the other side.
In a wooden bowl he placed them,
Shook and jostled them together,

Threw them on the ground in front of him,
Thus exclaiming and explaining:
"All the pieces are red side up,"
And one great Kenabeek standing
On the shiny side of a brass coin,
On a polished Ozawabeek;
"One hundred thirty-eight are counted."
Then he shook the pieces again,
Shook and jostled them together,
Threw them on the ground in front of him,
Still exclaiming and explaining:
"Both of the great Kenabeeks are white,"
White the Ininewug, the wedge-men,
Red are all the other pieces;
"Five tens and an eight are counted."
Thus he taught the game of chance,
Thus it displayed and explained it,
Running through its various possibilities,
Various changes, various meanings:
Twenty curious eyes stared at him,
Full of eagerness, they stared at him.
"Many games," said old Iagoo,
"Many games of skill and chance"
Have I observed in various nations,
Have I performed in different countries.
He who plays with old Iagoo
Must have very nimble fingers;
Though you believe yourself to be so skilled,
I can defeat you, Pau-Puk-Keewis,
I can even teach you lessons
"In your game of Bowl and Counters!"
So they sat and played together,
All the elderly men and the young men,

Played for dresses, weapons, wampum,
Played until midnight, played until morning,
Played until the Yenadizze,
Until the clever Pau-Puk-Keewis,
They had been stripped of their treasures.
Of the finest of all their clothing,
Shirts made of deerskin, robes made of ermine,
Belts of wampum, crests of feathers,
Weapons of war, pipes and pouches.
Twenty eyes stared at him with wild intensity,
Like the eyes of wolves glared at him.
Said the fortunate Pau-Puk-Keewis:
"In my wigwam I am lonely,"
In my travels and experiences
I need a companion.
I would gladly have a Meshinauwa,
An attendant and pipe-bearer.
I'm willing to risk all these gains.
All these clothes piled around me,
All this wampum, all these feathers,
On a single throw will venture
"Everyone against that young man over there!"
It was a young person of sixteen years old,
It was a nephew of Iagoo;
Face-in-a-Mist, the people called him.
As the fire burns in a pipe bowl
Dusky red beneath the ashes,
So beneath his shaggy eyebrows
The eyes of old Iagoo glowed.
"Ugh!" he replied with great intensity;
"Ugh!" they all replied, every single one of them.
The old man grabbed the wooden bowl.
Tightly in his skeletal fingers

Onagon gripped the deadly bowl,
Shook it violently and with rage,
Made the pieces ring together
As he threw them down in front of him.
Red were both the great Kenabeeks,
Red the Ininewug, the wedge-men,
Red the Sheshebwug, the ducklings,
Black the four brass Ozawabeeks,
White alone the fish, the Keego;
Only five pieces were counted!
Then the smiling Pau-Puk-Keewis
Shook the bowl and threw the pieces;
Gently he threw them up into the air,
And they collapsed around him, scattered in all directions;
Dark and bright flow the Ozawabeeks,
Red and white the other pieces,
And standing tall among the rest
One Native American was standing,
Even as the cunning Pau-Puk-Keewis
Stood alone among the players,
"Five tens! The game is mine!"
Twenty eyes stared at him with fierce intensity.
Like the eyes of wolves glared at him,
As he turned and walked away from the wigwam,
Followed by his Meshinauwa,
By the nephew of Iagoo,
By the tall and graceful young man,
Carrying in his arms the prize money,
Shirts made of deerskin, robes made of ermine,
Belts of wampum, pipes and weapons.
"Carry them," said Pau-Puk-Keewis,
Pointing with his fan of feathers,
"To my wigwam far to the east,"

"On the dunes of Nagow Wudjoo!"
Hot and red with smoke and gambling
Were the eyes of Pau-Puk-Keewis
As he stepped out into the fresh air
Of the Pleasant Summer Morning.
All the birds were singing cheerfully,
All the small streams flowing quickly,
And the heart of Pau-Puk-Keewis
Sang with joy just as birds sing,
Beat with triumph like the streamlets,
As he walked through the village,
In the early gray of morning,
With his fan made of turkey feathers,
With his feathers and clusters of swan's down,
Until he reached the most distant wigwam,
Reached Hiawatha's lodge.
Silent and deserted it was;
No one greeted him at the entrance.
No one came to welcome him;
But the birds were singing around it,
In and out and around the doorway,
Hopping, singing, fluttering, feeding,
And high up on the ridge-pole
Kahgahgee, the King of Ravens,
Sat with blazing eyes, and, shrieking,
Flapped his wings at Pau-Puk-Keewis.
"Everyone has left! The lodge stands empty!"
Thus spoke Pau-Puk-Keewis,
In his heart planning trouble
"Cautious Hiawatha has departed,"
Gone is the foolish Laughing Water,
Gone is Nokomis, the old woman,
"And the lodge is left unguarded!"

By the neck he grabbed the raven,
Spun it around himself like a rattle,
Like a medicine bag, he shook it,
Strangled Kahgahgee, the raven,
From the highest point of the tepee
Left its lifeless body hanging,
As an insult to its master,
As a taunt to Hiawatha.
With quiet footsteps, he stepped inside.
Around the lodge in chaotic disarray
Scattered the household items around him,
Heaped together in disorder
Wooden bowls and clay pots,
Robes made from buffalo and beaver fur,
Pelts of otter, lynx, and ermine,
As an insult to Nokomis,
As a taunt to Minnehaha.
Then Pau-Puk-Keewis departed,
Whistling, singing through the forest,
Whistling cheerfully to the squirrels,
Who from the hollow branches above him
Dropped their acorn shells on him,
Singing cheerfully to the forest birds,
Who emerges from the leafy darkness
Responded with an equally cheerful song.
Then he climbed the rocky headlands,
Looking over the Gitche Gumee,
Positioned himself at their highest point,
Waiting full of joy and playful trouble
The Return of Hiawatha.
Lying flat on his back, he remained there;
Far below him, the waters splashed.
The dreamy waters splashed and flowed gently.

Far above him, the heavens stretched endlessly across the sky.
Swam through the spinning, dreamlike heavens;
Around him, things hovered, fluttered, and rustled.
Hiawatha's mountain chickens,
A flock swept and wheeled around him in unison,
Almost brushed him with their wings.
And he killed them while lying there,
Killed them by the tens and twenties,
Threw their bodies down the headland,
Threw them on the beach below him,
Until finally Kayoshk, the sea-gull,
Positioned on a rocky cliff above them,
"It is Pau-Puk-Keewis!" they shouted.
He is killing us by the hundreds!
Send a message to our brother,
"Send word to Hiawatha!"

Chapter XVII:
The Hunting of Pau-Puk-Keewis

Full of anger was Hiawatha
When he arrived in the village,
Found the people in a state of confusion,
Heard of all the wrongdoings,
All the spite and the trouble,
Of the Cunning Pau-Puk-Keewis.
His breathing came hard through his nostrils.
Through clenched teeth, he buzzed
and muttered under his breath.
Words of anger and resentment,
Hot and buzzing, like a hornet.

"I will slay this Pau-Puk-Keewis,"
"Kill this troublemaker!" he said.
"The world isn't as vast and expansive as it seems,"
The path isn't as harsh and difficult as it seems.
That my anger will not reach him,
"My revenge will never touch him!"
Then they quickly left in pursuit
Hiawatha and the Hunters
On the trail of Pau-Puk-Keewis,
Through the forest, where he traveled through it,
To the headlands where he rested;
But they could not find Pau-Puk-Keewis,
Only in the trampled grasses,
In the blueberry bushes,
Found the couch where he had rested,
Found the imprint of his body.
From the lowlands far below them,
From the Muskoday, the meadow,
Pau-Puk-Keewis, turning backward,
Made a gesture of defiance,
Made a mocking gesture;
And Hiawatha cried out loudly,
From the summit of the mountains:
"The world is not so long and wide,"
The path isn't as harsh and difficult as it seems.
But my anger will catch up with you,
"And my vengeance shall reach you!"
Over rock and over river,
Through bushes, undergrowth, and forest,
Ran the cunning Pau-Puk-Keewis;
Like an antelope, he leaped forward.
Until he reached a small stream
In the middle of the forest,

To a quiet and peaceful stream,
That had spilled beyond its boundaries,
To a dam built by the beavers,
To a pond of quiet water,
Where the trees stood knee-deep in water,
Where the water lilies floated,
Where the tall grasses swayed and murmured softly.
On the dam stood Pau-Puk-Keewis,
On the dam made of tree trunks and branches,
Through the cracks in which water gushed out,
Over whose summit the stream flowed.
From the depths below, the beaver emerged,
Gazed with two magnificent eyes filled with amazement,
Eyes that appeared to be asking a question,
At the stranger, Pau-Puk-Keewis.
On the dam stood Pau-Puk-Keewis,
Over his ankles flowed the small stream,
The bright and silvery water flowed,
And he spoke to the beaver,
With a smile, he spoke in this way:
"O my friend Ahmeek, the beaver,
Cool and pleasant is the water;
Let me jump into the water,
Let me find rest there in your dwellings;
"Change me into a beaver too!"
Cautiously replied the beaver,
With caution, he responded:
"Let me first consult the others,"
"Let me ask the other beavers."
Down he sank into the water,
He sank heavily, like a stone sinking.
Down among the leaves and branches,
Brown and matted at the bottom.

On the dam stood Pau-Puk-Keewis,
Over his ankles flowed the small stream,
Water gushed through the cracks beneath him,
Smashed against the rocks below him,
Spread serene and calm before him,
And the sunshine and the shadows
Fell in scattered spots and flashes of light upon him,
Fell in small glittering patches,
Through the swaying, rustling branches.
From the depths below, the beavers emerged,
Silently above the surface
Rose one head and then another,
Until the pond appeared to be filled with beavers,
Full of black and shining faces.
To the beavers Pau-Puk-Keewis
Spoke pleadingly, saying these words:
"Your home is truly delightful,"
O my friends! and safe from danger;
Can't you, with all your cleverness,
All your wisdom and scheming,
"Change me into a beaver too?"
"Yes!" replied Ahmeek, the beaver,
He was the King of all the beavers,
"Let yourself slide down among us,"
"Down into the tranquil water."
Down into the pond among them
Pau-Puk-Keewis sank silently;
Black became his deerskin shirt,
Black were his moccasins and leggings,
In a broad black tail behind him
Spread his fox-tails and his fringes;
He was transformed into a beaver.
"Make me large," said Pau-Puk-Keewis,

"Make me large and make me larger,"
"Larger than the other beavers."
"Yes," the beaver chief replied,
"When you enter our lodge below,
In our wigwam we will make you
"Ten times larger than the others."
Thus into the clear, brown water
Pau-Puk-Keewis sank silently:
Found the bottom covered over
With the trunks of trees and branches,
Stockpiles of food for the winter,
Stockpiles and reserves stored against the famine;
Found the lodge with its curved entrance.
Leading into spacious chambers.
Here they made him grow bigger and bigger,
Made him the largest of all the beavers,
Ten times larger than the others.
"You will be our ruler," they said;
"Chief and King of all the beavers."
But Pau-Puk-Keewis had not been there long
Sat in state among the beavers,
When a voice of warning came
From the guard at his post
In the water-flags and lilies,
"Here is Hiawatha!"
"Hiawatha with his hunters!"
Then they heard a cry above them,
Heard shouting and trampling.
Heard a crashing and a rushing,
And the water all around and over them
Sank and was pulled down into swirling currents,
And they knew their dam was broken.
On the lodge's roof the hunters

Jumped, and shattered it completely;
The sunshine streamed through the crack.
The beavers leaped through the doorway,
Hid themselves in deeper water,
In the channel of the small stream;
But the mighty Pau-Puk-Keewis
Could not pass beneath the doorway;
He was swollen with arrogance and gluttony.
He was bloated like a balloon.
Through the roof, Hiawatha looked,
Cried aloud, "O Pau-Puk-Keewis
Vain are all your craft and cunning,
Vain your manifold disguises!
"I know you well, Pau-Puk-Keewis!"
With their clubs they beat and bruised him,
Beat poor Pau-Puk-Keewis to death,
Crushed him like corn being ground to meal,
Until his skull was shattered into fragments.
Six tall hunters, lean and agile,
Carried him home on poles and branches,
Carried the beaver's body;
But the ghost, the Jeebi within him,
Thought and felt as Pau-Puk-Keewis,
Still lived on as Pau-Puk-Keewis.
And it fluttered, fought, and struggled,
Waving here, waving there,
As the curtains of a wigwam
Wrestle with their leather straps made from deer hide,
When the winter wind is blowing;
Until it pulled itself together,
Until it rose up from the body,
Until it assumed the shape and characteristics
Of the Cunning Pau-Puk-Keewis

Vanishing into the forest.
But the cautious Hiawatha
Saw the figure before it disappeared,
Saw the form of Pau-Puk-Keewis
Glide into the soft blue shadow
Of the pine trees in the forest;
Toward the squares of white beyond it,
Toward an opening in the forest.
Like a wind, it rushed and gasped for breath,
Bending all the branches in its path,
And behind it, as the rain arrives,
The footsteps of Hiawatha approached.
To a lake with many islands
The breathless Pau-Puk-Keewis arrived,
Where among the water lilies
Pishnekuh, the brant, were sailing;
Through the clumps of reeds drifting,
Navigating through the reed-covered islands.
Now they raised their wide black beaks,
Now they dove underwater,
Now they grew dark in the shadow,
Now they gleamed brightly in the sunlight.
"Pishnekuh!" shouted Pau-Puk-Keewis,
"Pishnekuh! my brothers!" he said,
"Transform me into a brant goose with feathers,"
With a gleaming neck and feathers,
Make me big, and make me even bigger,
"Ten times larger than the others."
Immediately they transformed him into a brant,
With two enormous and dark wings,
With a chest that was smooth and curved,
With a bill like two enormous paddles,
Made him bigger than the rest,

Ten times larger than the largest,
Just as, shouting from the forest,
On the shore stood Hiawatha.
Up they rose with shouts and noise,
With a whirring sound and the beating of wings,
Rose up from the marshy islands,
From the water-flags and lilies.
And they said to Pau-Puk-Keewis:
"When you're soaring, don't look down,"
Take careful notice and do not look downward.
In case some unexpected misfortune should occur,
"Before some terrible disaster strikes you!"
Fast and far they fled to the north,
Fast and far through mist and sunshine,
Fed among the marshlands and wetlands,
Slept among the reeds and rushes.
On the next day as they traveled,
Carried and lifted by the South wind,
Carried forward by the South wind,
Blowing fresh and strong behind them,
Rose a sound of human voices,
A commotion erupted from below them.
From the lodges of a village,
From the people miles beneath them.
For the people of the village
Watched the flock of brant geese with amazement,
Saw the wings of Pau-Puk-Keewis
Soaring high up in the sky,
Wider than two doorway curtains.
Pau-Puk-Keewis heard the shouting,
Recognized Hiawatha's voice,
Knew the outcry of Iagoo,
And, forgetting the warning,

Drew his neck in and looked downward,
And the wind that blew behind him
Caught his mighty fan of feathers,
Sent him spinning and tumbling downward!
All in vain did Pau-Puk-Keewis
Struggle to regain his balance!
Spinning around and around and downward,
He looked at the village in turn
And in turn the flock above him,
Saw the village drawing closer,
And the flock moving farther away,
Heard the voices growing louder,
Heard the shouting and the laughter;
Saw no more the flocks above him,
Only saw the earth beneath him;
Dead out of the empty heaven,
Dead among the shouting people,
With a deep, mournful sound,
Shot down the goose with damaged wings.
But his soul, his spirit, his shadow,
Still survived as Pau-Puk-Keewis,
Took on the shape and appearance once more
Of the handsome Yenadizze,
And once again went rushing forward,
Hiawatha followed close behind,
Crying: "The world is not so wide,"
The journey isn't so long and difficult.
But my anger will catch up with you,
"But my revenge will reach you!"
And so close he came, so close to him,
That his hand was reaching out to grab him,
His right hand to grab and hold onto him,
When the clever Pau-Puk-Keewis

Spun around and whirled in circles,
Stirred the air into a whirlwind,
The dust and leaves swirled around him in a dancing motion,
And amid the swirling currents
Jumped into a hollow oak tree,
Changed himself into a serpent,
Gliding out through roots and debris.
With his right hand Hiawatha
Struck forcefully against the hollow oak tree,
Tear it apart into fragments and pieces,
Left it lying there in pieces.
But it was useless; for Pau-Puk-Keewis,
Once again in human form,
Full in sight ran on before him,
Swept away in gusts and whirlwinds,
On the shores of Gitche Gumee,
Westward by the Big-Sea-Water,
Came to the rocky headlands,
To the Pictured Rocks of sandstone,
Looking out over the lake and landscape.
And the Old Man of the Mountain,
He the Spirit of Mountains,
Opened wide his rocky doorways,
Opened wide his deep abysses,
Providing Pau-Puk-Keewis with Shelter
In his dark and gloomy caverns,
Welcoming Pau-Puk-Keewis
To his dark sandstone retreat.
There stood Hiawatha outside,
Found the doorways closed against him,
With his mittens, Minjekahwun,
Carved massive caves into the sandstone,
Shouted loudly with a voice like thunder,

"Open! I am Hiawatha!"
But the Old Man of the Mountain
The door remained closed, and no response came.
From the quiet sandstone cliffs,
From the dark rocky depths.
Then he lifted his hands toward heaven,
Called out desperately to the storm,
Called Waywassimo, the lightning,
And the thunder, Annemeekee;
And they arrived under the cover of night and darkness,
Sweeping down the Big-Sea-Water
From the far-off Thunder Mountains;
And the trembling Pau-Puk-Keewis
Heard the footsteps of the thunder,
Saw the red eyes of the lightning,
Was afraid, and crouched and trembled.
Then Waywassimo, the lightning,
Struck the entrances of the caves,
With his war club, he struck the doorways,
Struck the protruding cliffs of sandstone,
And the thunder, Annemeekee,
Shouted down into the caverns,
"Where is Pau-Puk-Keewis!" they called out.
And the cliffs collapsed, and underneath them
Dead among the rocky ruins
Lay the cunning Pau-Puk-Keewis,
Lay the handsome Yenadizze,
Killed while in his human form.
His wild adventures had come to an end.
His tricks and playful antics had come to an end.
Ended all his craft and cunning,
Ended all his mischief-making,
All his gambling and his dancing,

All his courting of the young women.
Then the noble Hiawatha
Took his soul, his ghost, his shadow,
Spoke and said: "O Pau-Puk-Keewis,
Never again in human form
Shall you search for new adventures;
Never again with jokes and laughter
The dust and leaves dance in whirlwinds;
But up there in the heavens
You will rise high and glide in endless circles;
I will transform you into an eagle,
To Keneu, the great war-eagle,
Chief among all birds with feathers,
"Chief of Hiawatha's chickens."
And the name of Pau-Puk-Keewis
Lingers still among the people,
Lingers still among the singers,
And among the storytellers;
And in winter, when the snowflakes
Swirl in whirlpools around the lodges,
When the wind blows in fierce, chaotic bursts
Over the smoke-flue pipes and whistles,
"Look," they shout, "here comes Pau-Puk-Keewis,
He is dancing through the village,
"He is gathering in his harvest!"

———————

Chapter XVIII:
The Death of Kwasind

Far and wide among the nations
Spread the name and fame of Kwasind;
No one dared to compete with Kwasind,
No one could compete with Kwasind.
But the mischievous Puk-Wudjies,
The envious Little People,
The fairies and the pygmies,
Plotted and conspired against him.
"If this hateful Kwasind," they said,
"If this great, outrageous fellow
Goes on like this for a little while longer,
Destroying everything he comes into contact with,
Tearing everything apart,
Filling the entire world with amazement,
What happens to the Puk-Wudjies?
Who will care for the Puk-Wudjies?
He will crush us underfoot like mushrooms,
Drive us all into the water,
Give our bodies to be eaten
By the wicked Nee-ba-naw-baigs,
"By the Spirits of the water!"
So the furious Little People
All conspired against the Strong Man,
All conspired to murder Kwasind,
Yes, to free the world from Kwasind,
The bold, domineering,
Heartless, arrogant, dangerous Kwasind!
Now this amazing strength of Kwasind
In his crown alone was seated;

In his crown too was his weakness;
There alone could he be wounded,
Nowhere else could a weapon pierce him,
Nowhere else could a weapon harm him.
Even there the only weapon
That could hurt him, that could kill him,
Was the seed-cone of the pine tree,
Was the blue cone of the fir tree.
This was Kwasind's deadly secret,
Known to no one among mortals;
But the clever Little People,
The Puk-Wudjies knew the secret,
Knew the only way to kill him.
So they collected pinecones together,
Collected pine cones from the pine tree,
Collected blue pinecones from the fir tree,
In the woods near Taquamenaw,
Brought them to the river's edge,
Piled them together in enormous heaps,
Where the red rocks from the edge
A rocky ledge extends out over the river.
There they waited in ambush for Kwasind,
The malicious Little People.
It was an afternoon in summer;
The air was extremely hot and completely still.
Very smooth flows the gliding river,
Motionless the sleeping shadows:
Insects sparkled in the sunlight,
Insects glided across the water's surface,
Filled the sleepy air with buzzing,
With a war cry that echoed far and wide.
Down the river came the Strong Man,
In his birch canoe came Kwasind,

Drifting gently with the flow
Of the slow-moving Taquamenaw,
Very sluggish due to the weather,
Very sleepy with the silence.
From the overhanging branches,
From the tassels of the birch trees,
The gentle Spirit of Sleep came down;
By his ethereal armies encircled,
His invisible companions,
The Spirit of Sleep, Nepahwin, arrived;
Like a polished Dush-kwo-ne-she,
Like a dragonfly, he hovered
Over the drowsy head of Kwasind.
To his ear came a murmur
As waves crash upon a seashore,
As of distant rushing waters,
As winds move through the pine trees;
And he felt it on his forehead
Strikes from small, weightless battle clubs,
Wielded by the drowsy armies
Of the Spirit of Sleep, Nepahwin,
As if someone were breathing on him.
At the first strike of their war clubs,
A drowsiness fell upon Kwasind;
At the second strike, they hit him.
Motionless his paddle rested;
At the third, before his vision
The landscape spun into darkness,
Kwasind was sleeping very deeply.
So he drifted down the river,
Like a blind person sitting upright,
Floated down the Taquamenaw,
Beneath the quivering birch trees,

Beneath the forested cliffs,
Beneath the military camp
Of the Pygmies, the Puk-Wudjies.
There they stood, all armed and waiting,
Threw the pine cones down at him,
Struck him on his muscular shoulders,
On his unprotected head, he struck him.
"Death to Kwasind!" was the sudden
War-cry of the Little People.
And he swayed sideways and fell down,
Sideways fell into the river,
Submerged beneath the slow-moving water
Headfirst, like an otter diving;
And the birch canoe, abandoned,
Drifted empty down the river,
The bottom curved and drifted upward:
Nothing more was seen of Kwasind.
But the memory of the Strong Man
Stayed for a long time among the people,
And whenever through the forest
The winter storm raged and roared with fury.
And the branches, tossed and troubled,
The ship creaked, groaned, and broke apart.
"Kwasind!" they shouted; "that is Kwasind!"
"He is collecting his firewood!"

———————

Chapter XIX:
The Ghosts

Never does the soaring vulture stoop
On his prey in the desert,
On the sick or wounded bison,
But another vulture, watching
From his elevated vantage point high above,
Witnesses the downward fall and pursues it;
And a third one chases after the second,
Coming from the invisible ether,
First a speck, and then a vulture,
Until the air grows dark with wings.
So disasters don't come one at a time;
But as if they were watching and waiting,
Watching each other's movements,
When the first one comes down, the others follow.
Follow, follow, gathering like a flock
Around their victim, sick and wounded,
First a shadow, then a sorrow,
Until the air becomes dark with anguish.
Now, across all the bleak Northland,
Mighty Peboan, the Winter,
Breathing on the lakes and rivers,
Into stone had changed their waters.
From his hair he shook off the snowflakes,
Until the plains were covered with whiteness,
One continuous level,
As if, bending down, the Creator
With his hand, he had smoothed them over.
Through the vast and mournful forest,
The hunter roamed on his snowshoes;

In the village, the women worked.
Crushed corn, or prepared the deerskin;
And the young men played together
On the ice, the loud ball game continues,
On the plain, snowshoes dance across the surface.
One dark evening, after the sun had set,
In her wigwam Laughing Water
Sat with old Nokomis, waiting
For the steps of Hiawatha
Returning home from the hunt.
On their faces, the firelight glowed brightly.
Painting them with streaks of crimson,
In the eyes of old Nokomis
Shimmered like moonlight on water,
In the eyes of Laughing Water
Glistened like the sun in water;
And behind them crouched their shadows
In the corners of the wigwam,
And the smoke curled in spirals above them
Climbed and squeezed through the chimney
flue filled with smoke.
Then the curtain of the doorway
From the outside, it was gradually raised;
The fire blazed more brightly for a moment,
And for a moment the smoke swirled away,
As two women quietly walked in,
Entered through the doorway without being invited.
Without any greeting,
Without any sign of recognition,
Sat down in the farthest corner,
Crouching low among the shadows.
From their appearance and their clothing,
Strangers seemed they in the village;

They were extremely pale and gaunt,
As they sat there feeling sad and quiet,
Shaking, hiding in the darkness.
Was it the wind blowing above the chimney flue,
Muttering down into the wigwam?
Was it the owl, the Koko-koho,
Hooting from the gloomy forest?
A voice spoke clearly in the silence:
"These are corpses dressed in clothing,"
These are ghosts that come to haunt you,
From the kingdom of Ponemah,
"From the land of the Hereafter!"
Hiawatha was now returning home
From his hunting in the forest,
With snow covering his hair,
And the red deer on his shoulders.
At the feet of Laughing Water
Down he threw his lifeless burden;
She thought he was nobler and more handsome,
Then when he first came to court her,
First, he threw the deer down before her,
As a sign of his hopes,
As a promise of the future.
Then he turned around and noticed the strangers.
Hiding, hunched down in the darkness;
Said to himself, "Who are they?"
"What strange guests has Minnehaha?"
But he didn't question the strangers,
Only spoke to welcome them
To his home, his meals, his hearth.
When dinner was ready,
And the deer had been divided,
Both the pale guests, the strangers,

Emerging from the darkness,
Grabbed the best parts,
Grabbed the white fat of the deer,
Set apart for Laughing Water,
For Hiawatha's wife;
Without asking, without thanking,
Eagerly devoured the morsels,
Darted back into the shadows
In the corner of the wigwam.
Not a word spoke Hiawatha,
Not a single movement did Nokomis make,
Not a gesture, Laughing Water;
Not a single change appeared on their faces;
Only Minnehaha softly
Whispered, saying, "They are starving;
Let them do whatever brings them the greatest joy;
"Let them eat, for they are famished."
Many days came and went,
Many nights shook off the daylight
As the pine tree shakes off the snowflakes
From the midnight of its branches;
Day by day the guests remain motionless
Sat there silent in the wigwam;
But at night, whether in stormy weather or under starlight,
They went forward into the forest.
Bringing firewood to the wigwam,
Gathering pinecones for the fire,
Always sad and always silent.
And whenever Hiawatha
Came from fishing or from hunting,
When dinner was ready,
And the food had been divided,
Emerging from their shadowy corner,

The pale guests arrived, the strangers,
Grabbed the finest parts
Set aside for Laughing Water,
And without criticism or doubt
Darted back into the shadows.
Never once had Hiawatha
By a word or look he corrected them;
Never once had old Nokomis
Made an impatient gesture;
Never once had Laughing Water
Displayed anger at the injustice.
All of this they had endured in silence.
That the rights of guest and stranger,
That the virtue of generosity,
By a glance might not be diminished,
By a word might not be broken.
Once at midnight Hiawatha,
Ever alert, ever vigilant,
In the tepee, softly illuminated
By the glowing embers that were still burning,
By the glimmering, flickering firelight
Heard a sighing, often repeated,
From his bed, Hiawatha stood up,
From his rough buffalo hides,
Pushed aside the deer-skin curtain,
Saw the pale guests, the shadows,
Sitting upright on their couches,
Crying in the quiet midnight.
And he said: "O guests! Why is it
That your hearts are so troubled,
That you cry so deeply in the middle of the night?
Has the old Nokomis perhaps,
Has my wife, my Minnehaha,

Hurt or upset you through cruelty,
"Failed in hospitable duties?"
Then the shadows stopped crying.
Stopped crying and grieving,
And they said, with gentle voices:
"We are ghosts of the departed,"
Souls of those who were once with you.
From the realms of Chibiabos
We have come here to test you.
We have come here to warn you.
"Cries of grief and lamentation"
Reach us in the Blessed Islands;
Cries of anguish from the living,
Calling back their friends who have passed away,
Sadden us with pointless grief.
Therefore, we have come to test you;
No one knows us, no one pays attention to us.
We are nothing but a burden to you,
And we see that those who have died
Have no place among the living.
"Think of this, O Hiawatha!"
Speak of it to all the people,
That from now on and forever
They no longer cry out with sorrowful wails
Bring sorrow to the spirits of the dead
In the Islands of the Blessed.
"Do not place such heavy burdens
In the graves of those you bury,
Not such a heavy load of furs and wampum,
Not such a heavy burden of pots and kettles,
For the spirits grow weak beneath them.
Only give them food to take with them,
Only give them fire to light them.

"Four days is the spirit's journey"
To the land of ghosts and shadows,
Four its lonely night encampments;
Four times their fires must be lit.
Therefore, when the dead are buried,
Let a fire burn as night draws near,
Four times on the grave be kindled,
That the soul during its journey
May not lack the cheerful firelight,
May not stumble around in the dark.
"Farewell, noble Hiawatha!"
We have tested you,
You have tested your patience to its limits.
By the insult of our presence,
By the outrage of our actions.
We have found you great and noble.
Fail not in the greater trial,
"Don't lose heart in the more difficult battle."
When they stopped, a sudden darkness
Fell and filled the quiet dwelling.
Hiawatha heard a rustling sound
As if garments were trailing behind him,
Heard the curtain of the doorway
Lifted by a hand he could not see,
Felt the cold breath of the night air,
For a moment I saw the starlight;
But he no longer saw the ghosts,
Saw no more the wandering spirits
From the kingdom of Ponemah,
From the land of the Hereafter.

———————

Chapter XX:
The Famine

Oh, the long and dreary winter!
Oh, the cold and harsh winter!
Ever thicker, thicker, thicker
Froze the ice on lake and river,
Ever deeper, deeper, deeper
The snow fell across the entire landscape,
The covering snow fell and drifted
Through the forest, around the village.
Barely from his buried dwelling
Could the hunter force a way through;
With his mittens and his snow-shoes
He walked through the forest in vain,
Searched for bird or beast and found none,
Saw no track of deer or rabbit,
In the snow, no footprints could be seen.
In the horrifying, shimmering forest
Collapsed, and lacked the strength to get back up,
Died there from cold and hunger.
Oh the famine and the fever!
Oh, the devastation of starvation!
Oh, the devastating power of fever!
Oh the wailing of the children!
Oh, the agony of the women!
All the earth was sick and starving;
Hungry was the air around them,
Hungry was the sky above them,
And the hungry stars in heaven
Like the eyes of wolves glared at them!
Into Hiawatha's wigwam

Two other guests arrived, equally silent
As the ghosts appeared, and just as gloomy,
Didn't wait to be invited
Did not negotiate at the entrance
Sat there without saying a word of welcome
In the seat of Laughing Water;
Gazed with weary eyes and sunken cheeks
At the face of Laughing Water.
And the leader said: "Look at me!"
"I am Famine, Bukadawin!"
And the other said: "Look at me!"
"I am Fever, Ahkosewin!"
And the beautiful Minnehaha
Trembled when they gazed at her,
Trembled at the words they spoke,
Lie down on her bed in silence,
Hid her face, but made no answer;
Lay there shaking, freezing, burning
At the way they looked at her,
At the terrifying words they spoke.
Forth into the empty forest
Hiawatha rushed forward in his madness;
In his heart was deadly sorrow,
In his face a stony firmness;
On his forehead, the sweat of anguish
Started, but it froze and did not fall.
Dressed in fur clothing and equipped with hunting gear,
With his powerful bow made of ash wood,
With his quiver filled with arrows,
With his mittens, Minjekahwun,
Into the vast and empty forest
On his snowshoes, he moved forward.
"Gitche Manito, the Mighty!"

He cried out with his face turned upward
In that painful moment of deep suffering,
"Give your children food, O father!"
Give us food, or we will die!
Give me food for Minnehaha,
"For my dying Minnehaha!"
Through the echoing forest,
Through the vast and empty forest
Rang that cry of desolation,
But no other answer came.
Then the echo of his crying,
Then the echo of the woodlands,
"Minnehaha! Minnehaha!"
All day long Hiawatha wandered
In that sorrowful forest,
Through the shadow of whose thickets,
In the pleasant days of summer,
Of that never forgotten Summer,
He had brought his young wife home.
From the land of the Dakotas;
When the birds sang in the thickets,
And the small streams laughed and sparkled,
And the air was filled with fragrance,
And the beautiful Laughing Water
Said in a voice that didn't waver,
"I will follow you, my husband!"
In the wigwam with Nokomis,
With those dark companions who kept watch over her,
With the Famine and the Fever,
She was lying, the Beloved,
She, the dying Minnehaha.
"Listen!" she said; "I hear a rushing,
Hear a roaring and a rushing,

Hear the Falls of Minnehaha
"Calling to me from a distance!"
"No, my child!" said old Nokomis,
"'It's the night wind in the pine trees!'"
"Look!" she said; "I see my father"
Standing alone at his doorway,
Calling to me from his tepee
In the land of the Dakotas!
"No, my child!" said old Nokomis.
"'It's the smoke that waves and beckons!'"
"Ah!" she said, "the eyes of Pauguk
Glare upon me in the darkness,
I can feel his cold fingers
Holding mine in the darkness!
"Hiawatha! Hiawatha!"
And the desolate Hiawatha,
Far away in the middle of the forest,
Miles away in the mountains,
Heard that sudden cry of anguish,
Heard the voice of Minnehaha
Calling to him in the darkness,
"Hiawatha! Hiawatha!"
Over endless, trackless snow-covered fields,
Under snow-laden branches,
Hiawatha hurried home,
Empty-handed, heavy-hearted,
Heard Nokomis moaning, wailing:
"Wahonowin! Wahonowin!"
Would that I had died in your place,
Would that I were dead as you are!
"Wahonowin! Wahonowin!"
And he rushed into the wigwam,
Saw old Nokomis moving slowly

Rocking back and forth and moaning,
Saw his lovely Minnehaha
Lying dead and cold before him,
And his heart was bursting inside him
Uttered such a cry of anguish,
The forest groaned and trembled,
That the very stars in heaven
Shook and trembled with his anguish.
Then he sat down, remaining still and silent.
On the bed of Minnehaha,
At the feet of Laughing Water,
At those willing feet, that never
More would eagerly rush to greet him,
Never again would they follow carelessly.
With both hands he covered his face,
Seven long days and nights he remained there,
As if in a trance, he sat there,
Speechless, motionless, unconscious
Of the daylight or the darkness.
Then they buried Minnehaha;
In the snow they made her a grave
In the deep and dark forest
Beneath the groaning hemlock trees;
Dressed her in her finest clothing
Wrapped her in her ermine robes,
Covered her with snow, like ermine;
Thus they buried Minnehaha.
And at night a fire was lit,
On her grave, fire was lit four times,
For her soul on its journey
To the Islands of the Blessed.
From his doorway Hiawatha
Saw it burning in the forest,

Illuminating the dark hemlock trees;
From his restless bed he rises,
From the bed of Minnehaha,
Stood and watched it at the doorway,
That it might not be extinguished,
Might not leave her in the darkness.
"Farewell!" he said, "Minnehaha!"
Farewell, O my Laughing Water!
All my heart is buried with you,
All my thoughts move forward with you!
Come not back again to labor,
Come not back again to suffer,
Where the Famine and the Fever
Exhaust your emotions and neglect your physical well-being.
Soon my task will be completed.
Soon I will follow in your footsteps
To the Islands of the Blessed,
To the Kingdom of Ponemah,
"To the Land of the Hereafter!"

Chapter XXI:
The White Man's Foot

In his cabin by a river,
Close beside a frozen river,
An old man sat there, feeling sad and alone.
His hair was as white as freshly fallen snow.
His fire burned dim and weak.
And the old man shook and trembled,
Wrapped in his Waubewyon,
In his worn white leather covering,

Hearing nothing but the storm
As it thundered through the woods,
Seeing nothing but the snowstorm,
As it spun and hissed and floated.
All the coals had turned white with ashes.
And the fire was slowly dying,
As a young man, walking with ease,
At the open doorway, he entered.
Red with the blood of youth, his cheeks glowed.
Gentle were his eyes, like stars in springtime,
His forehead was bound with grasses;
Tied together and decorated with fragrant grasses,
On his lips was a beautiful smile,
Filling the entire lodge with sunlight,
In his hand he held a bunch of blossoms
Filling the entire lodge with sweetness.
"Oh, my son!" the old man cried out,
"Happy are my eyes to see you."
Sit here on the mat beside me,
Sit here beside the fading embers,
Let us spend the night together,
Tell me about your unusual experiences.
Of the places you have visited;
I will tell you about my skill and courage.
"Of my many miraculous acts."
From his pouch he pulled out his peace pipe,
Very old and oddly designed;
Made of red stone was the pipe-head,
And the stem a reed with feathers;
Filled the pipe with willow bark,
Placed a burning coal upon it,
Gave it to his guest, the stranger,
And began to speak in this way:

"When I breathe out around me,
When I breathe upon the landscape,
Motionless are all the rivers,
"The water becomes as hard as stone!"
And the young man replied with a smile:
"When I breathe out around me,
When I breathe upon the landscape,
Flowers bloom across all the meadows,
"Singing, onward rush the rivers!"
"When I shake my gray hair,"
The old man said with a dark frown,
"All the land is covered with snow;"
All the leaves from every branch
Fall and fade and die and wither,
For I breathe, and look! they are gone.
From the waters and the marshes,
Rise the wild goose and the heron,
Escape to faraway places,
For I speak, and behold! they cease to exist.
And wherever my footsteps wander,
All the wild animals of the forest
Hide themselves in holes and caves,
"And the earth becomes as hard as flint!"
"When I shake my flowing ringlets,"
The young man said with a gentle laugh,
"Warm, welcome showers of rain fall,"
Plants raise their heads in joy,
Back to their lakes and marshes
Come the wild goose and the heron,
The swift swallow darts homeward like an arrow,
Sing the bluebird and the robin,
And wherever my footsteps wander,
All the meadows sway with flowers,

All the forests echo with music,
"All the trees are thick with leaves!"
While they were speaking, the night came to an end:
From the far-off lands of Wabun,
From his gleaming lodge of silver,
Like a warrior dressed and decorated with paint,
The sun came and said, "Look at me."
"Gheezis, the great sun, behold me!"
Then the old man fell silent and could not speak.
And the air became warm and pleasant,
And sweetly upon the wigwam
Sang the bluebird and the robin,
And the stream began to murmur,
And the fragrance of growing grass
Through the lodge drifted gently.
And Segwun, the young stranger,
More clearly in the daylight
Saw the icy face before him;
It was Peboan, the Winter!
From his eyes, tears were flowing.
As streams flow from melting lakes,
And his body shrank and withered
As the blazing sun rose higher,
Until it faded into the air,
Until it disappeared into the ground,
And the young man saw before him,
On the hearthstone of the wigwam,
Where the fire had burned and produced smoke,
Saw the first flower of spring,
Witnessed the beauty of springtime,
Saw the Miskodeed in bloom.
Thus it was that in the Northland
After that unprecedented coldness,

That unbearable Winter,
When spring arrived with all its magnificent beauty,
All its birds and all its blossoms,
All its flowers and leaves and grasses.
Sailing on the wind toward the north,
Flying in large flocks, like arrows,
Like massive arrows fired through the sky,
Passed the swan, the Mahnahbezee,
Speaking almost like a human being;
And in long lines swaying, curving
Like a bowstring that suddenly breaks apart,
The white goose came, Waw-be-wawa;
And in pairs, or flying alone,
Mahng the loon, with resounding wings,
The blue heron, the Shuh-shuh-gah,
And the grouse, the Mushkodasa.
In the thickets and the meadows
The bluebird, the Owaissa, sang out,
On the Summit of the Lodges
Sang the robin, the Opechee,
In the shelter of the pine trees
Cooed the pigeon, the Omemee;
And the grieving Hiawatha,
Speechless in his boundless grief,
Heard their voices calling to him,
Stepped out from his dark doorway,
Stood and gazed into the heaven,
Gazed upon the earth and waters.
From his travels far to the east,
From the eastern lands where dawn breaks,
From the radiant land of Wabun,
Now Iagoo returned home,
The great traveler, the great boaster,

Full of fresh and unusual adventures,
Marvels many and many wonders.
And the people of the village
Listened to him as he told them
Of his amazing adventures,
Laughing, he answered him like this:
"Ugh! it is indeed Iagoo!"
"No one else sees such amazing things!"
He had seen, he said, a water
Bigger than the Big-Sea-Water,
Broader than Lake Superior,
Bitter so that no one could drink it!
The warriors looked at each other.
The women looked at each other,
"It cannot be so!" he said with a smile.
"Kaw!" they said, "it cannot be so!"
Over it, he said, over this water
A magnificent canoe arrived with wings,
A canoe with wings came flying,
Larger than a forest of pine trees,
Taller than the tallest tree-tops!
And the elderly men and the women
Looked at each other and giggled;
"Caw!" they said, "we don't believe it!"
From its mouth, he said, to greet him,
Waywassimo came, bringing the lightning,
Came the thunder, Annemeekee!
And the warriors and the women
Laughed out loud at poor Iagoo;
"Caw!" they said, "what stories you're telling us!"
In it, he said, came a people,
In the great canoe with wings
A hundred warriors came, he said;

All their faces were painted white.
And their chins were covered with hair!
And the warriors and the women
Laughed and shouted in mockery,
Like the ravens perched on the treetops,
Like the crows perched on the hemlock trees.
"Caw!" they said, "what lies you're telling us!"
"Don't think that we believe them!"
Only Hiawatha did not laugh,
But he spoke seriously and replied
To their mocking and their ridicule:
"Everything Iagoo tells us is true;"
I have seen it in a vision,
Seen the great canoe with wings,
Seen the people with white faces,
Witnessed the arrival of this bearded man
People of the Wooden Ship
From the regions of the morning,
From the radiant land of Wabun.
"Gitche Manito, the Mighty,
The Great Spirit, the Creator,
Sends them here on his mission.
Sends them to us with his message.
Wherever they move, before them
Swarms of stinging flies, the Ahmo,
The bee swarms, the maker of honey;
Wherever they walk, beneath them
Springs a flower unknown among us,
Springs the White-man's Foot in blossom.
"Let us welcome, then, the strangers,"
Greet them as our friends and brothers,
And the heart's right hand of friendship
Give them when they come to visit us.

Gitche Manito, the Mighty,
Said this to me in my vision.
"I also saw in that vision"
All the secrets of the future,
Of the distant days that shall be.
I gazed upon the western borders
Of the unknown, crowded nations.
All the land was filled with people,
Restless, struggling, working hard, striving,
Speaking many languages, yet feeling
But one heartbeat in their chests.
In the forests, their axes echoed loudly,
Smoke rose from their towns throughout all the valleys,
Over all the lakes and rivers
Rushed their great canoes of thunder.
"Then a darker, more depressing vision"
Drifted past me, hazy and resembling clouds;
I saw our nation scattered,
All forgetful of my advice,
Weakened, fighting against one another:
Saw the remnants of our people
Sweeping westward, wild and sorrowful,
Like the scattered clouds of a storm,
"Like the withered leaves of Autumn!"

———————

Chapter XXII:
Hiawatha's Departure

By the shore of Gitche Gumee,
By the gleaming Great Water,
At the entrance of his tepee,
In the pleasant summer morning,
Hiawatha stood and waited.
All the air was filled with freshness,
All the earth was bright and joyful.
And before him, through the sunshine,
Westward toward the neighboring forest
Passed in golden swarms the Ahmo,
Passed the bees, the honey-makers,
Burning, singing in the sunshine.
Bright above him shone the heavens,
The lake stretched out flat before him;
From its depths jumped the sturgeon,
Sparkling, flashing in the sunshine;
On the edge of the great forest
Stood reflected in the water,
Every treetop cast its shadow,
Motionless beneath the water.
From Hiawatha's forehead
Gone was every trace of sorrow,
As the mist rises from the water,
As the mist rises from the meadow.
With a joyful and triumphant smile,
With a triumphant expression,
As if someone experiencing a vision
Sees what is to be, but is not,
Hiawatha stood and waited.

Toward the sun his hands were lifted,
Both palms pressed flat against it,
And between the separated fingers
The sunshine fell on his features,
Speckled with light across his bare shoulders,
As it falls and speckles an oak tree
Through the split leaves and branches.
Over the water floating, flying,
Something in the hazy distance,
Something in the morning mist,
Emerged and rose from the water,
Now it appeared to be floating, now it appeared to be flying,
Coming closer, closer, closer.
Was it Shingebis the diver?
Or the pelican, the Shada?
Or the heron, the Shuh-shuh-gah?
Or the white goose, Waw-be-wawa,
With water dripping and flashing,
From its shiny neck and feathers?
It was neither a goose nor a diver,
Neither pelican nor heron,
Over the water floating, flying,
Through the gleaming mist of morning,
But a birch canoe with paddles,
Rising and falling on the water,
Dripping, flashing in the sunshine;
And within it came a people
From the far-off land of Wabun,
From the most distant regions of dawn
The Black-Robe chief arrived, the Prophet,
He the Priest of Prayer, the Pale-face,
With his guides and his companions.
And the noble Hiawatha,

With his hands raised high above him,
Raised high as a gesture of welcome,
Waited, filled with joy and excitement,
Until the birch canoe with paddles
Scraped against the gleaming stones,
Stranded on the sandy shore,
Until the Black-Robe chief, the Pale-face,
With the cross resting on his chest,
Landed on the sandy shore.
Then the joyful Hiawatha
Cried out loudly and spoke in this way:
"Beautiful is the sun, O strangers,"
When you've traveled so far to visit us!
All our town peacefully awaits your arrival.
All our doors are open to you;
You will enter all our wigwams,
For the heart's right hand we give you.
"Never has the earth bloomed so joyfully,"
Never has the sun shone so brightly,
As they shine and blossom today
When you've traveled so far to visit us!
Never has our lake been so peaceful.
Nor so free from rocks and sandbars;
For your birch canoe as it passes by
Has cleared away both the rocks and the sandbar.
"Never before had our tobacco
Such a sweet and delightful taste,
Never the wide leaves of our cornfields
Were so beautiful to look at,
As they appear to us this morning,
When you've come so far to see us!
And the leader of the Black-Robes responded,
Spoke with a slight stutter,

Speaking words that are still unfamiliar:
"Peace be with you, Hiawatha,"
Peace be with you and your people,
Peace found in prayer, and peace found in forgiveness,
"Peace of Christ, and joy of Mary!"
Then the generous Hiawatha
Led the strangers to his home,
Seated them on buffalo hides,
Seated them on ermine fur.
And the thoughtful old Nokomis
Brought them food in bowls made of basswood,
Water carried in birch bark cups,
And the calumet, the peace pipe,
Filled and lit for their smoking.
All the elderly men in the village,
All the warriors of the nation,
All the Jossakeeds, the Prophets,
The magicians, the Wabenos,
And the Medicine-men, the Medas,
Came to welcome the strangers;
"It is well," they said, "O brothers,"
"That you've traveled so far to visit us!"
In a circle around the doorway,
With their pipes, they sat quietly without speaking.
Waiting to see the strangers,
Waiting to receive their message;
Until the Black-Robe chief, the Pale-face,
From the wigwam came to greet them,
Stammering slightly in his speech,
Speaking words that are still unfamiliar;
"That's good," they said, "O brother,
"That you've come so far to see us!"
Then the Black-Robe chief, the Prophet,

Delivered his message to the people,
Told the purpose of his mission,
Told them of the Virgin Mary,
And her blessed Son, the Savior,
How in faraway places and times
He had lived on earth just as we do;
How he fasted, prayed, and worked hard;
How the Jews, the accursed people,
Mocked him, whipped him, crucified him;
How he got up from the place where they had put him,
Walked again with his disciples,
And ascended into heaven.
And the chiefs responded, saying:
"We have listened to your message,"
We have heard your words of wisdom,
We will think about what you tell us.
It is good for us, brothers,
"That you've traveled so far to visit us!"
Then they stood up and left.
Each person returned home to their wigwam,
To the young men and the women
Told the story of the strangers
Whom the Master of Life had sent them
From the radiant land of Wabun.
Heavy with the heat and silence
Grew the afternoon of Summer;
With a sleepy sound the forest
Whispered around the sweltering tent,
With the gentle sound of sleeping water
Rippled on the beach below it;
From the cornfields, sharp and endless
Sang the grasshopper, Pah-puk-keena;
And the guests of Hiawatha,

Exhausted by the summer heat,
Slept in the hot tent.
Slowly across the shimmering landscape
As evening's dusk and coolness fell,
And the long and level sunbeams
Shot their spears into the forest,
Breaking through its protective barriers of darkness,
Hurried into every hidden trap,
Searched every thicket, valley, and hollow;
Still the guests of Hiawatha
Slept in the quiet tepee.
From his place, Hiawatha stood up,
Said goodbye to old Nokomis,
Spoke in whispers, spoke in this way,
Did not wake the guests who were sleeping.
"I am going, O Nokomis,"
On a long and distant journey,
To the gates of the Sunset.
To the regions of the home-wind,
Of the Northwest Wind, Keewaydin.
But I'm leaving these guests behind me,
In your protection and care I leave them;
See that no harm ever comes near them.
See that fear never troubles them.
Never danger nor suspicion,
Never lacking food or shelter,
"In the lodge of Hiawatha!"
He went forth into the village.
Said goodbye to all the warriors,
Said goodbye to all the young men,
Spoke persuasively, spoke in this manner:
"I am leaving, O my people,
On a long and distant journey;

Many months and many years
Will have come, and will have vanished,
Before I return to see you again.
But I leave my guests behind me;
Listen to their words of wisdom,
Listen to the truth they tell you,
The Master of Life has sent them
"From the land of light and morning!"
On the shore stood Hiawatha,
Turned around and waved his hand as he left;
On the Clear and Bright Water
Launched his birch canoe for sailing,
From the pebbles of the shore
Pushed it out into the water;
"Westward! westward!" he whispered to it.
And it shot forward with incredible speed.
And the evening sun setting
Set the clouds ablaze with crimson light,
Burned the broad sky, like a prairie,
Left upon the calm water
One long path and trail of magnificence,
Down whose stream, like flowing down a river,
Westward, westward Hiawatha
Sailed into the fiery sunset,
Sailed into the purple vapors,
Sailed into the evening twilight:
And the people from the margin
Watched him floating, rising, sinking,
Until the birch canoe appeared to be lifted
High into that sea of splendor,
Until it disappeared into the mist
Like the new moon slowly, slowly
Disappearing into the purple horizon.

"Farewell forever!" they said.
"Farewell, O Hiawatha!" he said.
And the forests, dark and lonely,
Moved through all their depths of darkness,
Sighed, "Farewell, O Hiawatha!"
And the waves upon the shore
Rising, rippling on the pebbles,
Sobbed, "Farewell, O Hiawatha!"
And the heron, the Shuh-shuh-gah,
From her dwelling places among the marshlands,
Screamed, "Farewell, O Hiawatha!"
Thus Hiawatha departed,
Hiawatha the Beloved,
In the glory of the sunset,
In the purple mists of evening,
To the regions of the home-wind,
Of the Northwest Wind, Keewaydin,
To the Islands of the Blessed,
To the Kingdom of Ponemah,
To the Land of the Hereafter!
Words to Know
Adjidau'mo, the red squirrel
Ahdeek, the reindeer
"Ahmeek", the beaver
Annemee'kee, the thunder
Apuk'wa, a bulrush
Baim-wa'wa, the sound of the thunder
Bemah'gut, the grapevine
Chemaun', a birch canoe
Chetowaik', the plover
Chibiabos, a musician and friend of Hiawatha;
ruler of the Land of Spirits
Dahin'da, the bull frog

Dush-kwo-ne'-she or Kwo-ne'-she,
the dragonfly
Esau, shame on you
Ewa-yea', lullaby
Gitche Gumee, The Big-Sea-Water,
Lake Superior
Gitche Manito, the Great Spirit,
the Master of Life
Gushkewau', the darkness
Hiawatha, the Prophet, the Teacher,
son of Mudjekeewis, the West-Wind and Wenonah,
daughter of Nokomis
Ia'goo, a great boaster and storyteller
Inin'ewug, men, or pawns in the Game of the Bowl
Ishkoodah', fire, a comet
Jee'bi, a ghost, a spirit
Joss'akeed, a prophet
Kabibonok'ka, the North Wind
Ka'go, do not
Kahgahgee', the raven
Kaw, no
"Kaween", absolutely not
Kayoshk', the Seagull
Kee'go, a fish
Keeway'din, the Northwest wind, the Home-wind
Kena'beek, a serpent
"Keneu," the great war-eagle
Keno'zha, the pickerel
Ko'ko-ko'ho, the owl
Kuntasoo: The Game of Plumstones
Kwa'sind, the Strong Man
Kwo-ne'-she, or Dush-kwo-ne'-she, the dragonfly
Mahnahbe'zee, the swan

Mahng, the loon
Mahnomo'nee, wild rice
Mom, the woodpecker
Me'da, a medicine man
Meenah'ga, the blueberry
Megissog'won, the great Pearl-Feather,
a magician, and the Spirit of Wealth
Meshinau'wa, a pipe-bearer
Minjekah'wun, Hiawatha's mittens
Minneha'ha, Laughing Water; wife of Hiawatha;
a waterfall in a stream flowing into the
Mississippi between Fort Snelling and the
Falls of St. Anthony
Minne-wa'wa, a pleasant sound, like the wind
in the trees
Mishe-Mo'kwa, the Great Bear
Mishe-Nah'ma, the Great Sturgeon
"Miskodeed", the Spring-Beauty, the Claytonia Virginica
Monda'min, Indian corn
Moon of Bright Nights, April
Moon of Leaves, May
Moon of Strawberries, June
Moon of the Falling Leaves, September
Moon of Snow-shoes, November
Mudjekee'wis, the West-Wind; father of Hiawatha
Mudway-aush'ka, the sound of waves breaking on a shore
Mushkoda'sa, the grouse
Nah'ma, the sturgeon
Nah'ma-wusk, spearmint
Na'gow Wudj'oo, the Sand Dunes of Lake Superior
Water spirits, supernatural beings of the water
Nenemoo'sha, sweetheart
Nepah'win, sleep

Nokomis, a grandmother, mother of Wenonah

No'sa, my father

Nush'ka, look! look!

Odah'min, the strawberry

Okahha'wis, the fresh-water herring

Ome'mee, the pigeon

Ona'gon, a bowl

"Opechee", the robin

Osseo, Son of the Evening Star

Owais'sa, the Blue-Bird

Oweenee, wife of Osseo

Ozawa'beek, a round piece of brass or copper used in the Game of the Bowl

Pah-puk-kee'na, the grasshopper

Pau'guk, death

Pau-Puk-Kee'wis, the handsome Yenadizze, the son of Storm Fool

Pe'boan, Winter

Pemmican, meat from deer or buffalo that has been dried and ground into powder

Pezhekee', the bison

Pishnekuh', the brant

Place it, hereafter

Puggawau'gun, a war club

Puk-Wudj'ies, small wild men of the forest; pygmies

Sah-sah-je'wun, rapids

Segwun', Spring

Sha'da, the pelican

Shahbo'min, the gooseberry

Shah-shah, long ago

Shaugoda'ya, a coward

Shawgashee, the crayfish

Shawonda'see, the South-Wind

Shaw-shaw, the swallow

Shesh'ebwug, ducks; pieces in the Game
of the Bowl

Shin'gebis, the diver, or grebe

Showain'neme'shin, pity me

Shuh-shuh-gah', the blue heron

Soan-ge-ta'ha, strong-hearted

Subbeka'she, the spider

Suggest to me, the mosquito

Totem, family coat of arms

Ugh, yes

Ugudwash, the sunfish

Unktahee, the God of Water

Wabas'so, the rabbit, the North

Wabe'no, a magician, a juggler

Wabe'no-wusk, yarrow

Wa'bun, the East-Wind

Wa'bun An'nung, the Star of the East, the Morning Star

Wahono'win, a cry of lamentation

Wah-wah-tay'see, the firefly

Waubewy'on, a white skin wrapper

Wa'wa, the wild goose

Waw-be-wa'wa, the white goose

Wawonais'sa, the whippoorwill

Way-muk-kwa'na, the caterpillar

Wenonah, the eldest daughter; Hiawatha's mother, daughter
of Nokomis

Yenadiz'ze, a lazy man and gambler; an Indian gentleman who
cared greatly about his appearance

THE END

Thank You For Reading

You've Just Read a Piece of the Greatest Library Ever Rebuilt

Thank you for reading.

This book is one of thousands we're restoring, reimagining, and translating as part of the **Modern Library of Alexandria** — a global movement to preserve and share humanity's most important ideas.

What was once lost to fire and time is now rising again — not just as memory, but as living, breathing knowledge, freely accessible to all.

What You Can Do Next:

- **Keep Reading.**

  Discover more legendary works — in beautiful print, audiobook, or digital form — at LibraryofAlexandria.com.

- **Build Your Own Library.**

  Every title is available as a paperback, hardcover, or collectible boxset — at true printing cost. Craft a personal library worthy of display.

- **Spread the Light.**

  Share this book. Tell others about the movement. Help us translate every timeless work into every language, so no reader is ever left behind.

By finishing this book, you've already taken part in something extraordinary.

Join us at LibraryofAlexandria.com

Together, we're rebuilding the greatest library the world has ever known.

With appreciation,

The Modern Library of Alexandria Team

Visit:
www.libraryofalexandria.com
Or scan the code below: